Artificial Intelligence:
Foundations for Business
Leaders and Consultants

Brian T. Lenahan

Aquitaine Innovation Advisors ■ **Toronto**

Artificial Intelligence: Foundations for Business Leaders and Consultants. Copyright © 2019 by Brian Lenahan. All rights reserved. Printed in the United States of America. For information, address Aquitaine Innovation Advisors publishing.

www.aquitaineinnovationadvisors.com

Designed by Brian T. Lenahan

Library of Congress Cataloging-in-Publication Data

Names: Lenahan, Brian T., 1963- author.
Title: Artificial Intelligence: Foundations for Business Leaders and Consultants / Brian Lenahan
Description: First edition. | Toronto : Aquitaine Innovation Advisors, 2019. |
    Includes bibliographical references and index.
Identifiers: ISBN 978-1-989478-00-4 (paperback) | ISBN 978-1-989478-01-1
    (ebook)
Subjects: LCSH: Human-machine systems. | Artificial Intelligence. |
    Automation.

Our books may be purchased in bulk for promotional, educational, or business use. Please contact your local bookseller, through www.Amazon.com or by email at www.aquitaineinnovationadvisors.com

First Edition: May 2019

10 9 8 7 6 5 4 3 2 1

Contents

Dedication

For my father, and my grandfathers, men who modelled incredible strengths for me to follow.

ACKNOWLEDGEMENTS

I want to thank those who continue to inspire my artificial intelligence journey including the McMaster AI Society, MaRS Discovery District, MIT CSAIL, the Starbucks morning crew, and my former TD Bank colleagues.

To my editors Deb Hanrahan, Rob Kowal, "Nick Bradshaw", Carlos Aguirre, my dear wife Michelle Griffith, and several others - thank you for helping me convert my speaking voice into a writing voice with a warm, humorous way to disparage the former.

I'm grateful for the support of those former managers who acknowledged my restless spirit for innovation and allowed me to experiment.

Many thanks to YouTube – my reward for doing a page of writing.

Finally, where would I be without family who by their very presence in person or from across the globe reach out and warmly share their excitement whenever I or my company achieves a new milestone.

Artificial Intelligence:

Foundations for Business Leaders & Consultants

Introduction

Artificial Intelligence is everywhere. In the online and traditional media, in corporate strategies, and in your own home. So how can you make sense of AI for your business? To help you on the journey, this book goes beyond merely a definition of Artificial Intelligence. It delves into a discussion of strategies, tools, vendors and trends to ensure that, as a consultant and/or business leader, you are competitive this year and into the future.

Artificial Intelligence: Foundations for Business Leaders & Consultants illustrates how to successfully embed artificial intelligence into both your clients' organization and your own. The book provides a simplified view of a complex topic enabling readers to leverage AI for their own competitive advantage. The goal of AI should not be to replace human interaction, but rather to improve these interactions, thereby taking our own human capabilities to the next level. Organizations can best equip themselves for the accelerating onslaught of AI and machine learning systems by learning to partner with them. *Artificial Intelligence: Foundations for Business Leaders & Consultants* will guide you through that learning and partnering process.

As an executive in a Top 10 North American financial institution, I witnessed the evolution of artificial intelligence within a large corporate environment. In our case, we were addressing the ever-increasing challenge of cybercrime through the analysis of Big Data, Machine Learning, and fraud identification techniques. Each of these are components of the artificial intelligence world.

The first credible approaches to artificial intelligence came to us through Alan Turing (who proposed the question "Can machines think?") and his contemporaries in the 1950's. We then progressed through a series of so-called "AI winters" where the hype of AI declined due to lack of tangible results. Today we find ourselves in a world of robotics, data proliferation, accelerating computing power, and increasing global investment. Company leaders have watched the evolution and today businesses of all sizes can take advantage of the benefits of artificial intelligence.

The challenge today for organizations is not simply an awareness of technology changes including AI. Their challenge is magnified by the simple fact that the pace of the change is accelerating exponentially. *Artificial Intelligence: Foundations for Business Leaders & Consultants* will direct your efforts in a way that allows you and your organization to keep pace.

The modern organization could have any one of a number of dominant issues. Overly expensive operations, the ineffective use of resources, data analysis challenges, less than satisfactory customer experiences or some other issue entirely. Artificial intelligence tools exist today to assist with these issues, providing opportunities to support human interaction, and of course for consultant, business leader and organizational success. The future holds even greater opportunities for artificial intelligence.

Why This Book & Why Now?

Three simple words. Promise versus execution. The divide between the promise of AI and the actual implementation of AI amongst most organizations today remains vast. In fact, if your organization is implementing some sort of AI initiative, you represent only 1 in 5 of your peers according to various surveys conducted in only the last year.

Current CEO's are justifiably uncomfortable in leading the implementation of AI within their organizations. They are confronted by a multitude of available technologies including AI, analytics, cognitive tech, and Internet of Things (IoT) driving interconnection. This quartet of options is now commonly referred to as elements of Industry 4.0. A 2018 Deloitte study found that, while many are optimistic about its value, just "14% of CXOs (Chief Executive Officers) are highly confident their organizations are ready to fully harness Industry 4.0's changes." The world needs informed business leaders and consultants to bridge the confidence gap. It needs you.

So how significant will AI become? According to Gartner (a global research firm) by 2020, 30% of CIO's will include AI in their top five investment priorities. In addition, 30% of new development projects will have AI components delivered by joint teams of data scientists and programmers.

Every industry has pioneers, early adopters, and laggards. Pioneers see the future. While early adopters can't necessarily see the future, they know it's coming, it portends change, and they adopt new thinking to stay alive. Finally, there are the laggards. They're not sure the business will ever change and are slow to accept significant change opportunities because they have always been successful just as they are. Unfortunately, because of the blistering pace of technological change, the gap will only expand in the next five years. Consequently, laggards will find it increasingly difficult to keep pace. In fact, Price Waterhouse Ccopers (PwC) 21st Annual Global CEO Survey found that in 2013 only 11% of CEO's feared losing technological edge due to the speed of technological change. In 2018, that number rose with a staggering 44% of CEO's now harbouring such fear.

It's not simply about knowing what to do, or how fast to do it. It's also about finding skilled employees and being able to afford their skyrocketing salaries. The same PwC study suggested CEO's were three times more concerned with the availability of skills over the next five years.

As a consultant or business leader, you are uniquely positioned to help businesses to execute on the promise of Artificial Intelligence. You can do so by providing rational strategies your client or organization can practically execute. You can also do so by modelling the behaviour in your own firms use of AI tools.

As of early 2019, there are very few resources for consultants and business leaders to make sense of AI and its challenges and its opportunities. That's why I wrote *Artificial Intelligence: Foundations for Business Leaders & Consultants*. If you are located near any of the global AI hubs, the number of potential clients or partners will only increase. Areas like Toronto/GTA/Waterloo/Montreal in Canada with institutes like Vector and MaRS, or any number of Chinese cities including Shenzhen have seen AI investment blossom. You can position yourself to harvest those potential clients.

Business leaders I've spoken to recently largely feel ill prepared to leverage the inherent value in AI. They don't understand the technology, the potential benefits and risks, the employee implications, or the effect on the company culture. Consultants can build those knowledge bridges well into the future. Business leaders can make the investment in themselves to take advantage of this burgeoning technology.

1

What is Artificial Intelligence?

Personally, I loved being a banker in North America. I was fortunate enough to work with some stellar leaders, peers and employees over a 22-year career. My observation and participation in such dynamic change in an otherwise stable industry was energizing. I have experienced the expansion both organically and through acquisition. This allowed me to introduce new technology, incorporate lean Six Sigma practices, increase the focus on the customer and innovate in processes and technology. These became consistent themes throughout my time within the industry.

When I retired from banking, I searched for something that aligned to the most exciting component of the journey – how innovation and disruption could be successfully tied to human activities. For me, the Massachusetts Institute of Technology (MIT) program was a natural choice to augment my experience. In 2018, MIT was ranked as one the best AI graduate programs in the world. MIT's Artificial Intelligence strategy program, encompassing a cohort of over 500 colleagues from around the globe, spoke powerfully to me. The program's focus on collective intelligence and the exploitation of the best of combined computer and human capabilities was compelling. This is a philosophy I can readily agree with but more on that later. Let's begin with what AI attempts to do...operate like the human brain.

Emulating the Brain

According to Popular Science and other sources, there are about 100 billion neurons in the human brain and roughly 40,000 synapses interconnecting those neurons – that's four sextillion connections – more than all the stars in the universe. Imagine trying to replicate the human brain through technology – that's artificial intelligence. Artificial neural networks model themselves on biological structure and function and every time new data or information flows through the network, it changes. Because the human brain learns, it creates new connections. Researchers have been trying to recreate the human brain through neural networks for decades, yet it's only been in the last decade that five key components have coalesced, namely:

1. Computer processing speed
2. Storage capacity (cloud)
3. More robust algorithms
4. Extensive investment
5. More broadly available talent

AI Defined

There is so much talk about artificial intelligence in the global media, so let's take a moment to provide some clarity around what AI actually is and the practical applications for it in our world. AI is a collective term for computer systems with particular objectives that can sense their environment, think, learn, and take action in response to what they're sensing and their objectives. AI researchers, consultants, business leaders, and dictionary authors all define AI differently. So here are some of the dominant definitions:

- "The capability of a machine to imitate intelligent human behavior. (Merriam Webster)
- "The theory and development of computer systems able to perform tasks normally requiring human intelligence, such as visual perception, speech recognition, decision-making, and translation between languages." (Oxford Dictionary)
- MIT says AI is a set of computational systems or models that behave (externally) like humans, human "thought" processes, behave intelligently, and rationally.

The definition of AI is evolving as it seems like every time a new advancement is introduced, it's no longer considered AI. Artificial Intelligence really has a future focused perception, and the definition will evolve.

Humans in the Loop

"In the long run, curiosity-driven research just works better... Real breakthroughs come from people focusing on what they're excited about." Geoffrey Hinton

AI, in terms of human interaction, can work in one of four ways:

- **Automated Intelligence**: When no human is in the loop, there can be automation of routine or non-routine manual and cognitive existing tasks, which is referred to as automated intelligence.

- **Assisted intelligence**: AI with a human in the loop. This is where AI systems assist humans in making decisions or taking actions, yet do not learn from the interactions. The focus of assisted intelligence is helping people to perform tasks faster and better.

- **Augmented intelligence** is where AI systems augment human decision making and continuously learn from their interactions with humans and the environment. Augmented intelligence helps people make better decisions.

- **Autonomous intelligence** can adapt to different situations acting without human intervention.

As humans and machines collaborate more closely, and AI innovations come out of the research lab and into the mainstream, the transformational possibilities are staggering.

The language of AI can be confusing but easily learned so trust me this book will enhance your comfort with the lingo. In fact, the appendix has more detailed definitions. Just keep in mind the story of the brain and how researchers are trying to emulate its capabilities.

General vs Narrow AI

"Despite all its successes, machine learning is still in the alchemy stage of science."
Pedro Domingos – Professor, University of Washington

If you think of "Terminator" the movie when you think of artificial intelligence, then what's on your mind is General AI, essentially being able to do all things humans can do. Super AI (the scary stuff Elon Musk talks about) is being able to do all the things a human can do, only better. According to the best predictions out there, Super AI is at least 50 years or more away. So, let's focus on the present day where narrow AI is the reality.

Narrow AI is doing a defined task, and only that task, better than humans. Today's artificial intelligence has often been described as "Narrow AI" because machines and software are programmed to perform very specific functions. A robot in a warehouse can't look after your grandmother at her home (checkout the movie *iRobot* as an example). A basic human activity is outside the capability of what is otherwise a wondrous machine. Remember, reaching that level is called "general AI" where the machine applies intelligence to any problem at near human level intelligence.

One of the most complex games ever invented by humans is a board game called "Go". Until recently humans reigned supreme. An artificial intelligence called Alpha Go, developed by Deep Mind, beat the World Master in 2018. Using reinforcement learning (where the AI plays games against itself) it taught itself how to play the game Go, and within 40 days was better than any human on the planet. Ironically, Alpha Go now competes with other AI platforms for game supremacy. Notwithstanding its "Go" expertise, Alpha Go can't play chess. It can't even play checkers because it was not programmed to do so. It's Narrow AI of a singular task focus. A human however can do both.

The Practical Side of AI

I like to think of AI in more tangible terms based on how the technology is being used. Here are some everyday uses of AI (as of 2019):

Netflix uses artificial intelligence to provide customers with recommendations on movie and TV show titles by using a learning algorithm which includes which shows you have watched before and applying a percentage probability that you will like a similar movie or TV show. That way, you'll keep watching and paying your monthly fees.

Amazon Alexa is a virtual assistant developed by Amazon originally used in the Amazon Echo and Echo Dot smart speakers. Alexa can perform voice interaction, play music, podcasts and audiobooks, create to-do lists, set alarms, and providing real-time information while controlling home automation devices. Alexa is available in 6 languages and over 100 million devices sold as of January 2019.

Sotheby's, announced in March 2018, announced the launch of Curate. Curate is a mobile augmented reality (AR) app replacing a home's virtual staging images from 2-D perception (photographs or clunky virtual reality imagery) with augmented reality. This allows potential buyers to see the house as their own before they even purchase the property.

Augmented reality, using displays that are worn in front of the eyes and overlay information onto the world in front of you providing a heads-up display, gives vital information to surgeons overlaid on the patient. This augmentation permits the surgeon to access information without having to look away from the operating field. As the technology matures it is also easy to anticipate 3-D anatomical information actually overlaid on top of the patient.

IBM's Watson offers AI for multiple analytics and conversational purposes. Imagine you are involved in a legal case between global multinationals. There could very likely be millions of documents, of which only a subset is currently relevant. Finding those relevant precedents is like finding a needle in a haystack, not to mention expensive and unwieldy. JPMorgan, for example, announced last year that it is using software called Contract Intelligence, or COIN, that can dramatically reduce the amount of time it takes to review legal documents. What would have had taken legal aides 360,000-man hours in the past now takes seconds when done by COIN.

A facial recognition system is a technology capable of identifying or verifying a person from a digital image or a video frame from a video source. There are multiple facial recognition system methodologies, however in general, they work by comparing selected facial features from faces within a database. It is also described as a Biometric Artificial Intelligence based application that can uniquely identify a person by analyzing patterns based on the person's facial textures and shape. Like the security option on a Samsung cellphone for opening the unit with your face.

As human beings, we express how we feel in many ways. We use language, we write, and we also make facial expressions. AI can be trained to differentiate between those forms of expression and apply a probability factor to its conclusion regarding how we feel about something (If you still watch cable in the 21st century, think of TV's The Big Bang Theory character Sheldon Cooper trying to assess whether someone is being sarcastic or not). Sentiment analysis is being used in retail stores, for example to better understand customer emotions when shopping for and deciding to make a purchase.

Waze is the world's largest community-based traffic and navigation app. Drivers in your area share real-time traffic and road info, saving everyone time and gas money on their daily commute. Waze helps you navigate through traffic using Waycare's artificial intelligence capabilities.

Waymo is an autonomous car company whose vehicles can guide themselves without human conduction. They combine sensors and software to control, navigate, and drive the vehicle. I personally enjoy driving, especially on the open road, but this kind of vehicle has become a reality and may change or even one day eliminate the "art" of driving. In the U.S., 29 states currently allow autonomous cars on the road with some sources arguing the cost of these vehicles will fall by 90% by 2025.

Microsoft (now a $1 Trillion market cap company) and their Azure Machine Learning system allows you to extract information from various data sets to identify patterns and increase the probability of success in predicting future outcomes. What it does not do is guarantee the future; rather it predicts the future with a greater reliability than without the software.

Study - Natural Language Programming or NLP

NLP refers to using machine learning and statistical analysis to simulate what humans can do innately. It can manipulate human language to extract meaning, generate text and more. For example, NLP can create a summary of a long document or series of documents (as in legal case reviews), translate languages, and detect fraudulent transactions or spam email. Steps in the NLP process include data ingestion, analysis, reasoning, generation, and then actionable insights.

Customer service is a particularly powerful example of where NLP can improve business operations. Customer satisfaction, or more often dissatisfaction, comes with data. Whether through surveys, voice recordings, emails or other media. The ability to analyse massive amounts of data from each medium through natural language programming offers leaders incredible insights. Beyond insights, NLP affords the ability to offer up chatbots or virtual voice assistants to deal with issues immediately and focus call center staff on priority issues or escalations. Speech recognition, and converting spoken language into text or vice versa, is improving daily. In fact, Alexa and Siri can recognize over 90% of the spoken word at present and respond in kind. Better than most humans.

Natural Language Programming leverages statistics to compare reams of phrases across the internet. It attempts to "understand" phrases using algorithms which simulate human understanding. Still NLP cannot completely replicate human understanding as yet. To put NLP in context, computers can act like Siri, holding a "conversation" but this only works if the exchange involves data that Siri has seen/heard before. When Siri is unable to understand the matter at hand, it's a parking lot item to solve for later, and the response is something like "I don't understand". So, like any good system, Siri stalls for time until it can gather more information. Engineers continue their work to improve the response for next time and the objective for NLP is to evolve to Natural Language Understanding or NLU where the algorithm understands human speech (regardless of language, syntax, tone, etc.) to mimic human conversation with true understanding.

NLP however has a place in today's world. There currently exists solutions which read, compare, and summarize large volumes of data, and create value added output. Legal software solutions are being leveraged for precedent work typically completed by junior legal employees over countless hours. The software goes further to help humans predict the likelihood of a case win for their client with increasing accuracy.

Business intelligence (the processing of large amounts of data into meaningful insights) has leaped ahead over the last decade due to the influence of Natural Language Programming under the auspices of academia and research organizations and there is more to come. While only $7 billion in market size today, NLP is expected to more than double by 2021.

How Does AI Work?

I began this book with the simple argument that AI was everywhere. Take a trip in your car, do an online search, or get a shopping recommendation from Amazon. When you do any of these things you're using artificial intelligence.

I promised this would not be a technical manual on AI. Having said that, understanding what goes on in the background is important. I believe that offering a black box full of algorithms is at minimum foolhardy, and at maximum risky to both to your reputation, and to your client's business.

I said earlier that AI tries to emulate the human brain. Human brains operate through neural networks, and that is what AI algorithms emulate. AI neural networks collect vast amounts of data, and process it into patterns, conclusions, and output. AI computer systems or network are composed of thousands of neurons, each of which processes a small amount of the data fed into the network. The neurons each make a decision, and in combination thousands of decisions are made, and then they are added together, albeit yet not in isolation. These neurons require training, which requires data. The more frequent and robust the training, the more accurate the network becomes as it encounters new information.

In the last few years, a new approach called reinforcement learning has prevailed which involves applying rewards (like adding +1 versus punishment where the computer is given a -1) to encourage the network to solve identified problems. Applying the proper training, the network frequently performs better than humans (including being able to consume vast amounts more data), within those narrow parameters (recall I mentioned narrow vs general AI).

Case Study - AI & Human Disabilities

AI uses are not limited to the corporate world. In fact, some of the most exciting research in AI relates to humans

26

and their disabilities. In fact, I am inspired everyday by my daughter for teaching the afflicted to do what we all take for granted. She, a Speech Language Pathologist or SLP, thinks nothing of taking the hand of an adult who has experienced a stroke, or brain injury, or child whose development has been slower than average, to make progress towards communicating again. Most of us are blessed with the ability to speak yet tend to take it for granted.

The power of AI, combined with the wisdom and compassion of an SLP, will soon touch these speech impaired friends, or family members. Let me set the scene. John is 48 years old and has recently had suffered a stroke. His motor skills aren't impaired. He can walk and move his arms. He cannot, however, speak without slurring. It's wonderful that you can understand every word of his conversational language. How? The baseball cap and pair of eyeglasses John is wearing has machine learning that has memorized millions of similar sounds, vibrations, thought patterns and its neural net can process these patterns and translate them into conversational English and output through the small speaker on the glasses. Further, the glasses can translate, in real time, his sounds or thoughts into any of dozens of languages transforming John into the hero whenever the family is on vacation.

The complete technology doesn't exist today (by the time you read this, though, it just might!), but the components of these glasses and cap are either available or could be available in the next decade. What an incredible experience for John, especially when he can speak to his daughter every day!

Why Adopt AI?

So, what are some of the reasons for adopting AI? According to a Statista study (Reason's for Adopting AI Worldwide 2017) the top-rated reasons are as follows:

- will allow us to obtain or sustain a competitive advantage - 84%;
- will allow us to move into new businesses – 75%;
- new organizations using AI will enter our market – 75%;
- incumbent competitors will AI – 69%;
- pressure to reduce costs – 63%;
- suppliers will offer AI-driven products and services – 61%;
- and customers will ask for AI-driven offerings – 59%.

So, are these reasons those applicable to you and/or your clients? Do the reasons sound similar to those of previous technologies? In my own start-ups customer discovery interviews, our customers were far more interested in the benefits we could bring them, than in the "AI-powered" nature of our solutions. Being clear on why you are adopting AI is as important as adopting it successfully.

Are Businesses Really Using Artificial Intelligence Today?

At Toronto Dominion Bank, (also known as TD Bank), a top 10 North American financial institution, I was part of the fraud team journey. Fraud analytics is at the forefront of analytics capability and banks have been working at this for over a decade. We leveraged both Robotic Process Automation (a non-thinking form of automation) and AI to create a solution to more effectively protect our customers. Inside yours or your clients' business there is some form of analytics. You must be clear on how closely aligned your analytics team is with the business and how much do they influence strategic decisions. Similarly, are they advancing capabilities including predictive and other forms of analytics?

Microsoft released a report in 2019 identifying increasing customer engagement as a major focus for the role that AI will play in business. If you're a mature, more advanced business, according to the study, 100% of this demographic said AI would help them win and/or retain more business, while 74% was the overall average. Impact is expected to come from "business areas that are entirely unknown today" (56%) and core business (65%). The same Microsoft report found that only 4% of companies were actively using AI in many processes, and 61% are in the planning process or piloting AI in some way. Inside the organization, IT related processes lead the way (47%). Research and development (36%) and customer service areas (24%) follow so watch for these areas for companies to focus on in 2019.

Whether it's natural language processing, machine learning, predictive analytics, or other advances, businesses are making use of AI technology. Large auditing firms are leveraging AI (including NLP, image recognition and drones) to review massive amounts of data, replacing junior auditors. Automotive companies are using AI to understand driver behaviour, improving safety for traditional and hybrid cars as well as setting the stage for fully autonomous cars. Energy firms employ AI to improve accuracy in drilling site selection. Hotel concierges offer recommendation capabilities incorporating AI technology for restaurants, activities, theatre and more. Yet another example of AI uses is in insurance firms' policy development, claims review and insurance purchase activities. AI is certainly pervasive today and its uses will only continue to grow.

The Pervasiveness of AI

How do we know that this is not just a lot of hype? Could this era be like many AI "winters" which have preceded it? Will the investment funding will dry up? Will the tech types will move on to other more lucrative ideas? Will the world move on as it has done at least 4 times before? How pervasive is AI in today's world?

In my view, the faster today's companies wake up to the real potential of AI, the better. In 2017, a factory in Dongguan, China replaced 90% of human employees with robots. Production rose by 250% while errors or defects dropped by 80%. Daunting yet practical proof there are scenarios where machines perform better than humans.

Companies are increasingly deploying or planning to deploy a variety of disruptive technologies including

- Internet of Things (IoT),
- AI,
- 3D Printing,
- Smart Robotics and
- Conversational interfaces (ie Chatbots).

A 2019 Gartner study suggested there were 14.2 billion objects connected in 2019 and 25 billion projected connects in 2022. It is only natural that the increase of connected devices has and will result in an increase in the amount of data produced. Consequently, increases in the use of artificial intelligence will support the analysis of the data and to help consider the potential future applications of this vast quantity of data.

Globally 16% of businesses are using AI today (according to the 2019 Deloitte Global CEO study). That investment is heavily skewed towards large businesses who have made big early investments in AI. Notwithstanding early large business investment, AI is becoming increasingly commoditized, particularly where sold as Software-as-a-Service (covered in Chapter 8) and as such is becoming more accessible to small and medium size businesses.

It is also true that AI usage differs widely by country. A 2019 PwC study showed 25% of Chinese companies widely use AI, versus only 5% in the US. Most American companies are running pilots but have yet to scale up like China and are falling behind. In 2018, Stephen Schwartzmann, CEO of Blackstone Group, donated $350 million towards a $1 billion school at MIT to focus on AI and related technologies for fear of falling behind other countries. To the same end, the United States President recently signed an Executive Order directing federal agencies to invest more in AI.

This year's World Economic Forum in Davos, Switzerland called out AI as one of the leading change agents globally. In another recent survey, done by Gartner, the maturity of AI application at companies has jumped considerably, although it should be noted that the technology still is in its infancy.

In this book, we will examine the benefits, the biases, the hype and the reality of AI. We will move beyond the ads and flashing lights delving into why despite historic false starts, AI is now poised for trillions of dollars of global investment, and why Canada, for example, is uniquely positioned to support AI for business. AI will not only change how we do business, but also the workplace itself. The very nature of jobs and skillsets will be redefined in the AI era (refer Chapter 7).

Do Small & Medium Businesses View AI the Same Way as Corporates?

A 2018 report by Vistage (a leading business performance and leadership advancement organization for small and midsize businesses or SMB's) found that "57.6% of small-midsized business CEOs believe advanced technologies will impact their businesses in the next year, with 29.5% of those indicating that AI will be one of the technologies that has the most impact." So, compared to other data you will read in this book, SMB CEO's trail those in corporate environments but increasingly understand the value of AI to their organizations. Today, only 13.6% of SMB CEO's said they are using AI in some fashion in their operations today.

SMB's are looking to leverage AI to improve predictive analytics for forecasting customer behaviour, automating routine tasks, managing inventories, and making customer experiences more individualized. 91% of all enterprises interviewed by Vistage expect AI to deliver new business growth by 2023. All categories of AI adopters are expecting AI to contribute to their new business growth in five years.

If you're a consultant to SMB's, you need to take notice of the increasing investment being made by these organizations. As a business leader, if you're not investigating the possibilities of AI for your organization, you should at least be aware that your competitors are and you might wonder if this is an instance where the laggards are in fact the losers?

A Brief History of Artificial Intelligence

"A.I. is more important than fire or electricity."

Google CEO, Sundar Pichai

Today, statements are being made like those of Sundar Pichai regarding the importance of AI, but let's cast our minds back to yesterday. The study of machine-based intelligence began in earnest in the 1950's with Alan Turing and his UK team. The most famous output of the Turing era was his test for computer intelligence, put simply, if a human, could determine within 5 minutes whether the entity was a computer or not. By 1956, a team of leading minds at Dartmouth University in New Hampshire had coined the term 'artificial intelligence'. In 1968, the movie 2001: A Space Odyssey proposed a computer-based intelligence called HAL 9000. Unfortunately, HAL tried to kill the inhabitants of the spacecraft it controlled. Not a stellar introduction to AI! By 1970, interest and funding for AI began to dry up, particularly in the US government given the lack of progress being made and the field experienced its first AI "winter".

Machine learning, or algorithms dedicated to specific problems providing new insights, began taking shape in the late 1970's beginning with supervised learning (covered in Chapter 9 and the Appendix). Oddly enough interest in artificial intelligence was renewed in 1984 with the release of the movie Terminator. Once again, a daunting form of intelligence bent on killing humans. By 1997, AI was being applied towards a significantly different purpose, playing chess. Deep Blue, IBM's artificial intelligence product, using machine learning of the millions of potential moves in the game, defeated World Champion Garry Kasparov over six games. Interest in AI was renewed.

A history of AI is not complete without mentioning Geoff Hinton – currently a lead scientist at Google Brain AI, and founder of the Vector Institute in Toronto – who is the so-called "Godfather of AI". Hinton's revolutionary 1986 paper with David Rumelhart and Ronald Williams, focused on a technique called back propagation or "backprop", the foundation of deep learning and reinforcement learning. Looking back on the last 10 years, this methodology has been behind the majority of AI achievements related to speech recognition, game playing and image recognition.

The exponential rise of AI technology in the last two decades can be attributed to 5 key factors:

- The emergence of smarter, modern-day algorithms.

- Easy access to a huge volume of data because of increased mobile usage, connected devices and sensors.

- Cloud technology enabling cheaper and easier access to large scale computing power and bigger storage.

- The availability of funding for AI related projects and research.

- The war being waged by governments like China, India, the US to lead in AI development and implementation.

By the year 2011, AI was being applied in the popular TV game show "Jeopardy". IBM's Watson, being fed billions of pieces of data, defeated two previous Jeopardy champions. Watson was a software platform able to ingest a clue in a natural language like English, including unusual elements like puns, to arrive at the correct answer. One of the human opponents, Ken Jennings, said in resignation, "I felt obsolete, I felt like a Detroit factory worker in the '80s seeing a robot that could now do his job on the assembly line. I felt like 'Quiz Show Contestant' was now the first job that had become obsolete under this new regime of thinking computers."

In the same year, 2011, as Watson was winning Jeopardy, Siri was making "her" way into the hearts and minds of Apple iPhone users. With a somewhat rudimentary understanding of language, Siri could respond to natural language questions and greetings. By 2012, it wasn't simply phones becoming "smart", it was automobiles as well. Experiments by Google and others with numerous sensors, and onboard computers allowed autonomous vehicles to navigate campuses and closed environments. In 2016, a new IBM program called DeepMind took on the world's best Go player. With an infinitely greater number of moves than chess, DeepMind programmers took a completely different route to winning Go that no previous human had considered.

Satya Nadella, CEO of Microsoft recently said "In 1969, when President Kennedy committed America to landing on the moon, the goal was chosen in a large part due to the immense technical challenge it posed and the global collaboration it demanded. In a similar fashion, we need to set a goal for AI that is sufficiently bold and ambitious, one that goes beyond anything that can be achieved through incremental improvements to current technology." Asking global governments and institutions to collaborate will be a historic effort, but suffice to say, interest in AI is not going away.

Let's now take a look at how disruption is changing the world.

3

The World of Digital Disruption

In early 2018, I was the Keynote Speaker at a conference in Toronto and the subject of my speech was "Thriving in Disruption". While the speech and audience discussion were peppered with the technical aspects and stories of disruption, it was the emotional aspects that people raised most actively and ardently. How they felt about these changes. How they accepted, rejected, considered, and evolved in their perspectives on disruption. They talked about the evolution of recruiting for example, including the impersonal AI voice on the other end of the phone or website. They spoke about the advent of the Internet, Wi-Fi, laptops, mobile phones and how despite their influence in changing the workplace, they appeared to pale in comparison to the advent of AI. On the flip side, they also shared the impact on teams of failed projects that were expected to revolutionize their industry yet fell far short.

As a consultant or business leader, this may be the most important lesson to learn from this entire book. You will certainly discover what's truly relevant about Artificial Intelligence to help your organization, and your clients reach its goals, but the journey demands your leadership on the human side of AI implementation as well. You need to understand and acknowledge the existing fears and anxiety that exist about being overwhelmed, being outpaced and being out-skilled. The fear that people's roles will change or they will flat out be replaced by a robot. Many of us are feeling the impact in the workplace as AI settles in to the business of today and the future. CEO's of the future will need to understand and manage these cultural impacts.

Harvard University's Clayton Christensen coined the term disruptive innovation more than 20 years ago in his book 'The Innovator's Dilemma'. Christensen's book is a business classic that explains the power of disruption and disequilibrium, why market leaders are often set up to fail as technologies and industries change and what incumbents can do to secure their market leadership for a long time. By 2015, Christensen commented in the Harvard Business Review that the "theory is in danger of becoming a victim of its own success." So, if nothing else, champion the balance of human and AI engagement.

Now, let's take a step back and begin with a brief description of the evolution of digital disruption.

Digital Disruption's Evolution

The journey of digital disruption begins with a view of the four Industrial Revolutions. Toward the end of the 18th century, the First Industrial Revolution occurred. The steam engine, and mechanical production in factories, replaced human workers. Productivity flourished. During the latter third of the 19th century we enter the 2nd Industrial Revolution. Electrical power, the assembly line, specialization of jobs, global communication all came into play. As a result, the movement of people and ideas flourished. We then fast forward to the early 1970's when electronics, information technology, automated processes, computers, and networks came into being. This was the 3rd Industrial Revolution.

Today we are engaged in the 4th Industrial revolution or Industry 4.0. So, what's new? Smart devices, the cloud, artificial intelligence, robots, driverless cars and trucks, big data, convergence, the possibility of singularity (the difficult to comprehend state where superintelligence will be developed by self-directed computers and will increase exponentially rather than incrementally).

Where do Disruptions Come From?

The myth about disruptions is that they simply emerge fully formed from the sky. They do not. They evolve over time with a long incubation period, followed by accelerated growth. Social media, and Internet of Things (IOT), are examples of disruption which are now traditional methods of the 21st century.

In May of 2018, I attended the Toronto Tech Summit at the MaRS Discovery District. Not unlike other tech conferences being held around the world, the banter between attendees was electric. Ideas being shared by presenters or panelists were debated, accepted or discarded, and shared broadly via Twitter in the blink of an eye. I have no doubt that more than one new idea for disruption surfaced from that very conference. I also have no doubt that new alliances, whether partnership or employment, were formed to bring those disruptive ideas to reality.

Disruption is now emanating from non-traditional sources. My son is currently a 4th year university student in a business co-op program. Having done several work terms in a finance environment, he wanted to build his own equities analysis software simply to see if he could do it. He learned the Python software program, found existing stock services, coded the program, and designed the output. It works – incredibly well. Built from the corner of his desk while attending university. The traditional approach is out the window. Next generation employees believe they can just do it themselves given the power of coding. Disruption will inevitably follow.

Recognizing Disruption

If you believe in the adage that the only constant is change, then as a consultant or business leader, how do you recognize that change in order to make decisions on how to act? More specifically, can you recognize it in an age of digital change occurring at hyper speed.

You've likely heard about Kodak, IBM PC's, Blackberry, or global taxi cab firms. These are companies that were disrupted by other companies or other technologies. The current Big Four of Apple, Google, Amazon and Facebook are quickly being joined by new entrants such as SpaceX, Nvidia and so many more.

Disruption is not new. It's old. What's new, and what's got people talking is how fast disruption is occurring. How can you keep up?

Gartner identifies at least five distinct types of disruption. When you don't have a clear objective and the disruption is unintended, you have "serendipitous" disruption such as Craigslist. Alternatively think about Uber's destructive power over traditional taxi markets – "destructive" disruption. If an organization is intentionally disrupting itself before they are disrupted by another party, that's "self-disruption". And then there's "offensive" and "defensive disruption" where a company reinvents itself to provide a solution to a business problem (ie offensive - the iPhone) or encounters competitive organizations it must defend against to maintain market ownership (ie Android).

Financial services have been under the disruptive lens for at least a decade now. In a recent Accenture PLC study of 80 bank executives in North America, almost 80% stated their organization was at risk if they did not deal with rapid innovation happening elsewhere by updating their own technology.

One of the leading authors and forecasters in this space is Daniel Burrus. He has written numerous books on innovation, predicting the future of organizations and technology. Burrus argues it is critical to anticipate disruptions before they disrupt.

How Do You Know When Disruption is Occurring?

My father in law is currently 79 years old. He has a floor cleaner robot - he calls it Robie. Robie does a great job of picking up dust, food particles, and the like so that my father in law and his wife don't have to step or bend down in their condo. A cleaning person used to do that specific function for them. No longer. Times change, and robots are not only on their way, they're here.

What does this mean to you and your clients? What are the warning signs for disruption? KPMG, a world leading consulting firm, will tell you there are five distinct warning signs starting with "it's getting harder to win". Gaining new customers or satisfying those you have is becoming more challenging. Who your customers are, what they do, and what they expect from you require you to alter course. Focus on the customers changing needs trumps any kind of brand loyalty.

Next, you will be seeing new faces in your competition. It won't likely be in large bites. They will be specialists eating away at the corners of your offering. Some call it niches. Regardless the disruptive element is apparent.

Third, you'll hear more and more about one of those niche companies gaining popularity for their previously quaint solution. Their innovation has produced a following and you'll need to decide if you're going to fight against them, or with them.

Fourth, customer reactions to your proposals may be changing. They may refer to your direct competition, but also to others in tangential industries who are transitioning into your space. You may now be reacting rather than being proactive. This then raises the question of whether you are being forced out of the space, or are you developing innovative processes and solutions to counter the disruption?

Finally, business models are under attack. Amazon introduced the Amazon GO retail model which excludes human intervention at the checkout. In fact, customers merely present their phone on entry, pickup what they want and scan on exit. The retail world will never be the same! Are you challenging the existing business model on a regular basis with the internal agility to shift as necessary?

In 2018, I interviewed Edwin Suarez, Director HR Talent & Innovation at a major oil company, and an MIT cohort colleague, about disruption and what approach to AI he was recommending to his leadership team. He responded "As you know, AI is a suitcase word, a toolkit if you wish, so we need to map business problems and/or opportunities to the right tool in that toolkit. In Oil & Gas, there are known use cases such as reducing unplanned downtime of production equipment installed on assets (wells) through analytics and machine learning. The same concept could be applied in the downstream sector of the industry (i.e. refineries). More innovative approaches are directed towards better predicting oil and gas production volumes. AI has the potential to create better models, specifically for shale, than the traditional physics-based models. The future, in my opinion, will be in integrating different tools like natural language and image recognition, neural networks, and machine learning to fully automate field operations."

One colleague I spoke to argued that since business leaders are often in the 50-65 age range, and that their familiarity level with AI is low, they are generally risk averse and not wishing to entertain a 'new' technology like AI. So, what can you as a consultant do to counter some of these types of barriers, if in fact, AI is the right solution? Speaking to a leadership team's primary objectives makes the AI conversation more palatable, particularly in an environment of competitive disruption.

"FLAG" Disruption

Take for example the disruptive power of the so-called "FLAG" companies – Facebook, LinkedIn, Amazon, and Google. Facebook, without benefit of a user fee, introduced the "like" function and changed the face of social interaction. Since 2006, when it was first launched as a university/college tool, it has become a global public forum with over 2.2 billion users (almost third of the planet). Facebook makes most of its revenue (over $56 billion as of 2019) from advertisements that appear onscreen. While Myspace was the first pervasive social platform, Facebook simply resonated with more users. Using likes, and follows, Facebook generated a new language that resonated with younger generations who today live by the number of subscribers they have on YouTube, and how many followers they have. Platforms like these have changed society in myriad of ways and they will continue to do so.

LinkedIn, purchased by Microsoft in 2016, has changed the way employees profile themselves, and are recruited. The majority of employees will be vetted via LinkedIn before they are offered an interview. Writing resumes, prepping for interviews, and getting other tips are part of the standard global HR process today. With over 500 million members in over 200 countries, LinkedIn generates the bulk of its revenues by selling information.

Amazon, originally an online bookseller has migrated to millions of products online, and more recently retail stores without human-staffed checkouts. Amazon has changed the way we buy and the way we get purchases delivered to our door. In 2015, Walmart was surpassed by Amazon as the most valuable US retailer (online exceeds brick and mortar) and second only to Walmart in terms of employer size. Amazon has gone on to multiple lines of business including AWS (Amazon Web Services) which upended the on-site server industry with a cloud platform, a key predecessor of AI for data storage and other capabilities.

Google. Everyone knows what Google does…in fact it's now a verb…to 'Google' is to search online. Yet up to 1998 (Google's founding) there was no such activity. Like Facebook, Google depends on advertising to survive as it does not apply fees to its service. Several other Google services also figure in the top 100 most visited websites, including YouTube and Blogger. Google was the most valuable brand in the world as of 2017, and third behind Amazon and Apple in 2018. According to some sources, Google.com is the most visited website in the world.

In 2019, 84% of online advertising revenues are owned by Facebook and Google, which makes it very difficult for other online sites publishers to gain a share of revenue to make their sites sustainable. The impact of just these four companies is so vast it's almost incredible.

Disruption Readiness

So, is disruption really part of investment decision making in the next five years? 73% of CEO's think so according to the Ernst & Young (EY) CEO Imperative 2017. 72 percent of US CEO's stated they were taking the lead to disrupt their industries before being disrupted by their competitors. KPMG's 2017 CEO Outlook reported CEO's were "actively working to disrupt their sectors, rather than waiting to be disrupted by the competition". Yet half of CEO's aren't well prepared to gain competitive advantage through disruption according to the EY study. In 2018, KPMG reported those CEO's continued to comment that they rely on "their own intuition" to make strategic business calls.

It all begins with purpose; Harvard Business School professor Clayton M. Christensen says: "Decide what you stand for, and then stand for it all the time."

When working with business leaders, the first issue we usually discuss is business purpose, priorities, problems or challenges. We never start with AI. AI can be the shiny object that business leaders want to talk about because they've read an article about it, talked to a competitor or heard about it at the club. But that path is generally

49

ineffective. Start with priorities. Those priorities often impacted by the disruption you're experiencing.

When consulting clients balk at the possibility of changing their core business because disruption is squarely imposing on their ecosystem, what do you do? Go back to the core business problem they are trying to solve and look at all the options available to determine if they can remain competitive.

If after reading the previous section, you see elements of disruption in your industry, or business, then refining your understanding of that disruption is crucial to being ready to address disruption. Case in point, in my interview with Edwin Suarez, HR Director, he recommended that business leaders "…look at the market capitalization of the top 5 companies in the world, which happen to be digital companies, and to look at other industries that used to believe they wouldn't be disrupted. The automotive industry is a great example where organizations underplay the role of digital capabilities and new technologies, like electric cars, and now are playing catch up." Those new organizations embracing agile approaches, digital transformation and disruptive technologies obtain competitive advantage and radical growth. 67% of investors actively seek those companies who embed disruptive innovation activities within their overall strategy projects even if they're risky and don't provide short term benefits.

Core Revenues Paradigm

Working in the financial services industry for more than two decades, I observed the importance of protecting core revenues. In 2000, our CEO quite rightly focused the bank's priorities on safer retail customers to the tune of 80% of the total revenue base. This lesser risk approach, during a period of corporate and bank failures, and derivative product explosion, made good fiscal sense, and today's version of the organization is much better for it.

So why bother innovating when core revenues are stable? Because disruption is inevitable, and how your organization adjusts is critical. For those who are familiar with McKinsey's work on current roles and how susceptible they are to automation, one of the least susceptible is professional services (PS). PS is a diverse set of roles including scientists, mathematicians, consultants and coaches using judgment, their Emotional Quotient or EQ, and creativity. In the financial world, robo-advisors are a reality, however they have a narrow focus, are generally without physical form and require the collaboration of a human advisor. In the consulting industry, consultants worried about being replaced by a robot with infinitely greater memory, calculating ability, and access to data sources, must still realize the value of human interaction to clients. The current state of AI technology remains in the realm of narrow AI. Those who will succeed in the disruptive future will be the best at integrating these two ecosystems – human and machine - into one powerful solutioning service while managing core revenues.

Technology Trends

Contrary to what many seem to think, you don't need to be a software engineer or computer scientist to be a leader in the digital revolution. More vital is the ability to match technological solutions with existing business problems in innovative ways. It is therefore critical to develop an understanding of the underlying forces and mechanics driving these trends is critical.

Key trends in the realm of digital transformation include real-time analytics, NLP, Business Automation, Customer Service Automation, Machine Learning, Data Visualization, Recommendation Engines, Smart Home and IoT. According to Forrester Research in 2017, the Internet of Things or IoT, AI interfaces and immersive experiences, network decentralization, and the changing role of human-machine collaboration were foremost, and they continue today. The autonomous smart device whether for consumer or business purposes will emerge with individualization capabilities and interaction made possible by the capabilities of IoT and artificial intelligence. Let's explore each.

Networks are increasingly becoming decentralized. With the advent of social media and new business models, networks like blockchain technologies (which are decentralized and fragmented) transition businesses from the traditional centralized systems. Traditional host systems are being replaced with cloud (offsite) platforms.

Human voice and action or gesture are becoming more prevalent as interface technology. Alexa and Siri, are recent examples of the elimination of typed or text communication. As immersive experiences like Augmented Reality, Virtual Reality and others emerge, the very nature of the human-machine interface will change. How often have you been in a situation where you cannot or prefer not to type in your online search request? You're not alone. By 2020, 50% of all online searches are expected to be through voice recognition technology. Whether through your car, smartphone, home virtual assistant or another device. Giving instructions using your voice will become commonplace. Communicating with a chatbot, a technology that permits voice or text interaction resulting in a conversation, takes the human-computer interaction a step further. Customer service desks are migrating in droves to a chatbot environment where often the consumer cannot discern the chatbot from a human voice.

Industries adopt AI at different speeds. The Global Center for Digital Business Transformation produces a graphic representation they refer to as the Digital Vortex. The concept is simple – the closer you are to the center, the faster that part of the vortex is spinning. For example, if you're in media, tech products and services, financial services, your environment is spinning (read 'changing') so rapidly it's hard to keep up with the integration of new AI ideas and tools. If you're in real estate or transportation or utilities, you're at the outside edge looking in, spinning very slowly. If you're in government, (as of 2018), you're barely part of the vortex. Consulting, a component of the professional services industry, is somewhere in the middle (number 8 of 15 identified in the vortex) suggesting significant room for opportunity as we will define in Chapter 5.

From a consumer perspective, every second, 900,000 people interact with Facebook, 452,000 of us post to Twitter, and 3.5 millions of us search for something on Google. This is happening so rapidly that the amount of data which exists is doubling every two years, and this growth (and the opportunities it provides) is referred to as Big Data. Big Data is a key driver of AI. The term Big

Data refers to large data sets that can be analysed for patterns through artificial intelligence algorithms. Big data has been a focus of organizations who have so-called "data lakes" or pools of data that criss-cross the organization. Just a few years ago only giant corporations would have the resources and expertise to make use of data at this scale. Yet as progress is made, smaller and smaller data sets can render patterns and therefore smaller organizations will be able to leverage AI for that purpose. Also, a movement towards "software-as-a-service" platforms, through solutions offered by companies like Microsoft, Amazon and IBM, have reduced the need for big spending on infrastructure. This explosion in data is what has made many of today's other trends possible and learning to tap into the insights will increase any firms' prospects in just about any field.

In what now seems like the "olden days", only computers could connect to the internet. Maybe, if they were very advanced, some phones could too. Today you can buy lightbulbs, refrigerators, cars, watches, kettles, thermostats and many other "smart", connected, objects. In industry, machines are being built to communicate with each other with less need for human input, in order to more efficiently carry out tasks in factories, warehouses and other environments. Intel forecasts that by 2020 there will be 200 billion devices connected to the internet. Data from these devices can help us to make better decisions about our lives (such as monitoring our exercise habits with fitness trackers) as well as in business. There are huge opportunities out there for those who are able to develop products and services based around this data. Collectively this trend is known as "Internet of Things" because it isn't just an internet of computers and phones anymore! The potential here is really only limited by one's imagination.

4

How Fast Are Things Really Changing?

"We always overestimate the change that will occur in the next two years. And [we] underestimate the change that will occur in the next 10. Don't let yourself be lulled into inaction." Bill Gates, The Road Ahead.

It was 2007 when I first noticed new Fintech players in the North American Financial Services industry. As an employee of a large North American bank, I observed with fascination that such small organizations were trying to disrupt such a significant part of the global economy with such deep roots and legacy. These small start-ups with a heavy focus on technology began creating offerings in the payments space initially to compete with debit cards. At the time, few traditional players felt threatened by these small entities. The explosion in the use of smartphones led to the increase in mobile banking, investing services and cryptocurrency. Financial services became even more accessible to the general public. According to CB Insights, a research firm, by 2018, over 1,700 fintech deals occurred worth almost $40 billion and activity outside the US, UK and China accounted for 39% of the deals. New annual highs were hit in the US for 659 deals and almost $12 billion in investments. With more areas in fintech ready for disruption, including "reg tech" or compliance type technology, 2019 is expected to be a very active year.

Digital Adoption Rates Are Accelerating

The speed of digital transformation is incredible and adoption rates are accelerating. It took 50 years from its' invention for consumers to globally adopt the landline for telephone communication. It took 10 years for the cellphone to reach the same level of adoption. The smartphone took five.

One hundred years ago, US Steel was the largest company in the world with a capital market value of $46.4 billion in 2017 dollars. Two other steel companies shared the top 10, along with oil, farm equipment, rubber and telephone companies. 50 years later in 1967, International Business Machines (IBM) topped the list at $256.6 billion while three oil companies, automotive, manufacturing, retail and a telephone company filled out the remaining 9 positions. Just two companies remained on the top 10 from 50 years prior. By 2017, the list of the largest companies in the world was indistinguishable from that of 1967.

Computer & software corporations ruled in 2017. Apple, a small computer company started in a garage in 1976 has reached almost a trillion dollars in market cap.

Alphabet, the parent company of Google, started in 1998, reaching over $850 billion in just 20 years. Microsoft ($644B), Amazon ($543B), and Facebook ($518B) all had over half-a trillion dollars in market cap value as of November 2017. One investment company (Berkshire Hathaway), one oil company (Exxon Mobil), one consumer goods company (Johnson & Johnson) and two banks (JP Morgan Chase and Wells Fargo) round out the list of 10 largest global entities. Recently Microsoft topped the $1 Trillion dollar mark; the second company to do so after Apple. The trends are obvious. Computer entities have assumed prominence due to the value of data. (It has often been said that "data is the new oil" – refer to Chapter 9). These entities are growing much faster than any time in the past.

The Speed of Change on the Internet

What a difference a year makes in the world of the Internet. In 2016, YouTube had 2.7 million views per minute globally. Within 24 months that grew to 4.3 million. Uber more than doubled the number of rides to over 3,800 per minute in 1 year. Google searches increased from 2.4 million to 3.7 million per minute in 2018. Facebook managed over 973,000 logins per minute, a 30% increase over 2016. Snapchat – well Snapchat truly illustrates the change occurring on the internet from text to graphic content. Snapchat went from 527,000 images shared per minute in 2016 to 6.9 million. Incredible growth over just 1 year.

As of April 2019, there were 3.5 billion active users of social media or 45% of our total planet population, and not surprisingly for the most part they were accessing that media on their smart phones.

Not every Internet-based application, though, evidenced such growth in 2018. Email, a somewhat mature technology, grew by only 4% to 187 million per minute. Apple App Store apps downloaded grew relatively less at just 10% consistent with the market saturation of their products. Twitter Tweets were essentially flat year over year. Building forecasts based on Internet usage are clearly not as easy as predicting last year's numbers with some growth. Building a business on the Internet is equally uncertain.

In 1992, when NBC's Katie Couric asked the question on live TV "What is the Internet?", it was not widely known and global internet traffic was 100GB a day. Five years later it was 100GB an hour. Five years after that in 2002, internet traffic was 100GB per second. In 2019, total internet traffic is estimated to be 52,000GB per second, with fixed connections speed increasing at 36% from 2018 to 2019.

Of the 7.7 billion people on the planet as of April 2019, 66% have mobile phones, 58% use the internet, 45% are active social media users, and the same percentage are active mobile social media users. No wonder most photos you see of urban areas show people walking around with their mobile phones (which represent two-thirds of all the devices on the planet).

Is Voice Making an Impact?

In 2019, Global Web Index, a survey firm, asked internet users between the ages of 16 and 64, how often they used voice search and voice commands during the previous 30 days. For those aged 16-24, almost half of them (48%) had done so. Similarly, in the 25 to 34 year-old range 47% reported using voice search or voice commands. The numbers drop off precipitously in higher age groups (29% for 45-54, and 22% for 55-64). Still, my favourite three words for my smartphone GPS on a busy traffic are "take me home!"

How Fast is AI Being Adopted?

MIT conducted a study where respondents were asked "to what extent will the adoption of artificial intelligence affect your organization's offerings today and five years from today. On average about 15% felt that AI would have a large impact today. That number grew to anywhere from

40% to 65% within just 5 years. The Public Sector not surprisingly lagged behind such industries as Technology, Media and Telecom, Consumer, and Financial & Professional Services but overall the increase in impact of AI over five years was six-fold.

What About the Innovation Adoption Cycle?

It's accelerating too! You may have seen the traditional bell-shaped chart that illustrates how the population views and acts on innovation. On the extreme left, the innovators themselves. They are joined next by the early adopters, followed by the early majority, then the late majority and finally the laggards. The vast majority of people extend from the later early majority to the laggards. In 2018, the bell curve has now shortened. With the exponential speed of change of business, if you are not part of the innovators, early adopters or the really early majority, it may be too late to be even part of the game.

Often innovators are part of an underground movement dissatisfied with the status quo and experimenting with new technology and business models. Their exploits are heard about by early adopters who seek out their innovations. Then comes the early majority, the later majority and finally the laggards (the final three groups who represent the vast majority). Consider one instance to illustrate the adoption of AI in Human Resources, specifically recruitment.

Case Study: Recruitment

In the world of Human Resources, the hiring of employees and contractors was often a paper-laden, human interaction dominated activity. While there remains a critical role for hiring managers in the process, the ability today to automate parts of the process has exploded. Those parts are many.

First let's break down the AI capabilities being applied to HR and Recruitment according to CognitionX, an AI advice platform. The following table illustrates some of the functions of an HR department.

Recruitment	Engagement & Recognition	Compliance and Reporting
Candidate sourcing	Payroll & benefits automation	Monitoring bias
Hiring process automation	Engagement monitoring	Supervision of employee activities
Agent-led video interviews		
Predicting new hire performance	**Separation/Retirement**	**Risk Management**
	Outplacement	Retention and attrition analytics
Learning & Development	Pension Administration	Absence and accident prediction
Onboarding	Alumni and boomerang hiring sourcing	Fraud Detection
Reference information		
Personal coaching	**Performance Management**	
	Objective setting	
	Capacity predictions	
	Predicting performance	
	Team fit psychometrics	

Now we can break these activities down into the level of potential automation, versus how much value is added with the human touch:

High Automation Potential/Low Value Added with Human Touch	Low Automation Potential/High Value Added with Human Touch
Resume Collection/Parsing	Data-driven story-telling
Offer Creation	Making the close
Nurture Marketing	Negotiation/Persuasion
Candidate propensity signals	Re-skilling
Assessment based on code depositories	Nuanced understanding of candidates
Candidate matching	needs
Pre-screening assessments	Understanding team culture
Candidate ranking	Community building
Interview scheduling/bots	Differentiated candidate experience
Database search relevancy	
Candidate sourcing	
De-duping databases	
Social profile aggregation	

So how do you select which to pursue first? There are several criteria to consider, including automation potential, level of complexity, cost, and potential benefits. You can make the decision or AI can make a recommendation as to how to approach the business problem.

Capgemini Consulting in 2017 produced an analysis of AI use cases comparing complexity and benefit. "Many firms miss the chance to implement low complexity and high benefit artificial intelligence use cases. This is the must do quadrant. 54% of the firm in this quadrant haven't implemented the suggested use case yet."

Do Case by Case – High Complexity, Low Benefits.	Need to Do – High Complexity, High Benefits	Can Do – Low Complexity, Low Benefits	Must Do – Low Complexity, High Benefits
• Tailoring AI to help developers create new tools • **Optimizing recruitment of top talent** • **Position matching** • **Identifying talent for training** • Sentiment analysis • Supply chain design • Personalized shopping experience • Anomaly detection • IT Compliance	• Audience targeting • Trading strategies • Personalized customer care • New product development • Voice recognition and authentication • Decision support • Image/video recognition	• Predictive maintenance • Programmatic media buying • Lead generation and tracking • Real-time bidding platforms • Churn detection • **Optimizing career path** • **Detecting high potential employees/lo performers**	• Analyze consumer behavior • Contextual/pr edictive customer care • Risk management • Network Security • Facial recognition • Chatbot/virtua l assistant • Reduce revenue churn • Product or services recommendati ons • Forecasting • Regulatory compliance • Fault detection

Recruitment is a great example considering the amount of AI advancement going on in the sector. When you think about AI, take two approaches. The simple and the complex. Let's start with the simple. AI is a toolkit meant to improve your business. Treat it like any other toolkit.

Now the complex. There are so many potential players, regulations, technical knowledge, channels, strategies/plans, processes involved in implementing AI that it can easily boggle the mind. That's why this book was published. To provide the business leader with a clearer path to AI success.

Consulting Strategies, Tools, Tips & Tactics

When I was putting my notes together for this book, the most difficult challenge I had was deciding what not to include. There is an overwhelming amount being written today about disruption, artificial intelligence, and technology. Imagine how overwhelming it is for your clients or your teams! This is one of the many reasons why they need you.

Show of hands how many people here have heard of RoboAdvisors? (Ok, virtually raise your hands). Right, so-called robots in the financial services industry? What about Robot-Consultants or Robo-Coaches? They're each possible, but will any of these replace humans completely. I would argue 'No" , and the rest of this book will tell you why.

What Do I Need to Know?

I'm an enthusiastic realist when it comes to technology. What motivates me is not the machine, but what it can do to help us solve problems. More sophisticated machines allow us to tackle more complex problems. The more complex the problem, the greater my interest.

I'm also extremely curious. Find me at a dinner party or Starbucks and I'm the first to search Google for the name of that actor in that show you saw 20 years ago. It may appear obsessive. I prefer highly curious. It's that attribute, curiosity, that often ranks near the top in the search for disruptive talent.

That profile certainly does not fit everyone in today's working world. As a consultant or business leader, you'll never have to understand artificial intelligence in depth. You don't have to know how exactly it works. That's less relevant to you. You don't have to be a data scientist or an analytics expert. You just have to know that there are AI-powered tools that do things you weren't capable of doing before which can now begin to inform your strategy.

As a consultant or business leader, what can you do to support AI initiatives and those charged with implementing them? Specifically, how do you identify where AI can add value? The answers you provide could conceivably range from providing information and resources all the way to implementing solutions? Which type of consultants (and business leaders) specifically would this apply to?

If you want to do business with corporate clients (by the way they employ 84% of independent consultants – see the end of this chapter), you can't avoid the subject of AI. This is especially true when you need to stand out from the competition. Corporate leadership teams are trying to navigate the immense change in technologies and train their people to use AI efficiently. That means they need outside experts who are following the trends and have their finger on the pulse of the best practices for using AI. Practical tips and anecdotes told in layperson's terms will wow your corporate prospects and build incredible opportunities to help them integrate AI. It will also allow you to help your clients leverage AI-powered sales tools to help position them as truly agile organizations.

In my organization, we teach consultants and business people how to optimize the use of AI tools to improve their effectiveness with clients, partners, and employees. For example, by combining the EQ capabilities of coaches with chatbots, the coaching client can receive a better experience during, and interim to, their coaching sessions. In one instance, the coach provided webinars, one-on-one sessions and wrote blogs on being overwhelmed. To augment those efforts, we designed a chatbot to support clients in situations when they were feeling overwhelmed and wanted a different outlet or conversation path to address those feelings. For consultants, we combine their ability to create and sustain relationships with clients with tools like IBM Watson Analytics to extend their analytics capabilities and shorten the time to solution. In terms of the role of AI - "Better" (so many ways to define that term!) is the goal, and AI's role, in my view, as noted earlier, is to combine with humans, wherein each contributes their capabilities or competencies to that goal.

How to Read Chapter 5

This chapter is one of lists. Lists to provide consultants with strategies, tools, tips and tactics to literally "run" up the AI learning curve and leverage optimum speed (defined in Chapter 6) to rapidly integrate AI into their offering. Let's start with why you might care.

Why Should Consultants Care About AI?

Consultants – why should they care about AI both for themselves but perhaps more importantly for the corporate clients who they're serving?

- If you care about remaining competitive.
- If you care about being efficient.
- If you care about operating in an environment where you understand the needs of clients or teams using or about to use AI.

"To the extent you aren't embracing it now, you're slowing down the ability to actually continue to scale in any market globally" according to the Alphabet (Google's parent company) CFO and increase the chances of an AI-ready company encroaching on your market.

Five "Must Haves" for Every AI strategy

AI strategy is my area of expertise, and I've seen these four "must haves" applied over and over again in technology projects, in white papers, and in case studies.

1. Buy-in from stakeholders (support & agreement, financial investment, etc.).

2. Right people – engineers, data scientists, analytics experts (coding, ML, domain knowledge).

3. Great data – attributable, accurate, accessible data.

4. Start by identifying a use case that is reasonable in size and consumes a lot of time (typically an administrative task) that no one likes to do.

5. Smart small. Gain successes then scale up.

When starting an AI project with a client, these five must-haves' go a long way towards increasing the probability of success from planning to implementation. As Kevin Kelly, a Wired magazine contributor says "The business plans of the next 1000 start-ups are easy to forecast: Take X & Add AI".

Is it Better to Innovate with Outside Help?

Boston Consulting Group (BCG) would offer you at least seven reasons why you should innovate externally (get help wherever you can and look broadly for it), namely new ideas, disruption protection, acceleration, collaboration, leadership, and assessment and identification of technology impact.

1. Finding the next big thing.
2. Avoiding disruption by unearthing emerging technologies and innovation trends.
3. Linking with start-ups and leading inventors to accelerate innovation.
4. Building networks of collaborators to stay on top of leading edge technology.
5. Assessing the impact of new technologies on the business.
6. Identifying the impact of new technologies on the business.
7. Attaining a position of technology leadership.

By consuming new information daily through online articles, blogs, websites you'll also be exposed to trend analysis, and who's winning the technology race. You will learn to separate soft trends (those that might happen) from hard trends (those that will happen) and integrating that analysis into an organizations strategy.

Borealis AI Approach

Borealis is an RBC Company, a global financial institution in Toronto, Canada. According to the company, they support "RBC's innovation strategy through fundamental scientific study and exploration in machine learning theory and applications. The team aims to develop state-of-the-art technology and supports academic collaborations with world-class research centres in artificial intelligence." Here's how they uniquely approach AI challenges:

- Research first then look for a business problem in a business unit to align with it.
- Researchers work on a problem they are interested in
- They approach business and find an opportunity to apply research
- Key Performance Indicators are discussed and monitored
- Requires a broad mandate for Borealis; leverages creativity

It's an atypical approach but it seems to be working for Borealis. There are an increasing number of AI research institutions across the globe and connecting with one of them on a unique business problem may prove very insightful with long term benefits for your firm.

Your Own Consulting Practice's AI Strategy

The guiding principle of this book is to understand AI, not from a technical programming or coding perspective, rather from a use case perspective. Use AI in your own business. AI is in every industry (notwithstanding some are slower than others) so every consultant or business person needs to understand, and leverage AI. Here's my list of key strategies and tactics (beyond the "five must haves" above) to leverage to make your consulting firm stand out in this AI world.

1. Roll out new concepts/tools/services out over time.
2. Gain wins with one mini-project and move to the next.
3. Bundle technologies.
4. Watch the hype cycle and develop a healthy obsession with technology.
5. Buy, borrow and/or build.
6. Get out there! Attend pitch competitions.
7. Get out there! Visit tech hubs and innovation centers and meet with curious people.
8. Get out there! Take a field trip to anywhere you can learn more about how technology is being used by your client's competitors or your own.
9. Develop an external relationship with universities, innovation hubs, research institutes.
10. Attend conferences to learn more like EMTECH (MIT) or AI World Forum
11. The large consulting firms (Deloitte, PwC, KPMG, EY) are sending their employees to institutions like MIT to learn about AI. What are you doing to

constantly learn? Where are you directing your clients to learn new skills or upgrade existing ones?

Consulting Case Study

Consider the case of Bluewolf, an IBM Company and a Salesforce Global Strategic Consulting Partner. By offering the Bluewolf suite of services, the company creates a value add offering to organizations of all sizes trying to implement Salesforce. They focus on speed to implementation (advisedly 30-60 days). They have been involved with 10,000+ Salesforce projects including Salesforce products like Customer Success Platform, Salesforce Sales Cloud, Salesforce Service Cloud, Field Service Lightning, Salesforce CPQ and Pardot.

Are SMB's really using the cloud? Some sources suggest the cloud adoption rate by US SMB's has increased 50 percent over the past four years, though the consulting industry offers surprisingly few options. Some business leaders report having to implement Salesforce themselves or alternatively rely on partners without a proven reputation. Bluewolf's suite approach is to offer pre-built solutions, interactive training, market frameworks, and a standard implementation methodology.

Comparing Vendors

It's always a great idea to get referrals for software solutions that work. Peers, or clients who have used a software solution can be very helpful in reducing the amount of time it takes to find the right one. When you don't have access to those sources, or when you're looking for a more robust analysis, there are numerous sites online that compare different vendors and their software platforms and applications. They are a ready source of independent validation and verification for AI tools in discovering which is optimal for yours or client's needs. Here are six of the most active sites:

1. Capterra - https://www.capterra.com
2. G2 Crowd - https://www.g2crowd.com
3. Software Advice - https://www.softwareadvice.com/ca/
4. GetApp - https://www.getapp.com
5. Salesforce AppExchange - https://appexchange.salesforce.com/
6. Predictive Analytics Today - https://www.predictiveanalyticstoday.com/top-predictive-analytics-software/

According to Joe Galvin, Chief Research Officer at Vistage Worldwide. "Early adopters are beginning to realize the benefits of automation and the deep insights harvested from big data. There is no need to become a data scientist or even to hire one. Small business owners can strategically identify and select business applications that have AI embedded in them and look for opportunities to automate the routine that will free their people for more creative work." When you are investigating AI software solutions for your own business or for your clients, a brief stop at one of these sites will reduce the time you consume.

10 AI Tools for Consultants

If you're asking me what specific tools we're talking about, here's a top 10 list for consultants including examples of vendors. The list is by no means exhaustive, nor promoted by me. You should consider the list directional only.

1. Research & Report Generation – Quill from Narrative Science
2. Prospecting scheduling/email communication – Outreach.io
3. Customer Service – chatbots built via Chatfuel.com
4. Prospecting/Lead Generation – Discoverleadgeneration.com
5. Presentation creation – beautiful.ai
6. Recruiting – Ideal.com
7. Predictive analytics – Microsoft Azure Machine Learning
8. Insights – IBM Watson
9. Meeting scheduling – Zoom.ai
10. AI Research – MIT Sloan Management Review

Business Owner Interviews

When you are interviewing business leaders or owners about their innovation approach, consider using the following questions: it's a lot like your typical consultant client interview, with a hint of AI.

Strategy & Vision

- What do you think are the primary strategic priorities and goals for your company over the next one year, three years, five years?
- Instead of looking for ways to bring AI into their business, SMBs can look for ways to use AI to execute on business strategy. What tasks could be automated? What key questions could be answered?
- What activities as CEO would you do to achieve success in these priorities?
- How do your priorities relate when faced with new entrants and existing competitors?
- How do you identify trends and opportunities?

Technology

- Like many companies you are experiencing changes in your operating environment due to continued digital transformation, the shifting patterns of content consumption and aggressive competitors. What have you done to implement technology improvements, e.g., platform integrations, new enterprise management systems?

- Can you share a time when you have had to expand a core product set through innovation, and particularly in a mobile environment?
- How would you bring greater innovation to the company?
- What innovations have you led at other businesses that are most germane?
- How do you handle data collection, management, and analysis? Do you treat data as your most valuable resource and have you established any systems that effectively collects the data that will inform decision making?
- How do you identify repetitive tasks? Do you think about whether an application could take the time and aggravation out of completing tasks by performing them automatically?
- What is the organizations tolerance for risk?

Teach Your Clients the Five Ways to Thrive in Disruption

In order to provide guidance to your clients in a period of disruption, like today, you can teach them to both REACH and CLIMB. These are concepts developed by my company, Aquitaine Innovation Advisors, through years of interacting with colleagues, peers, clients and our extended network. There are two sets of acronyms, REACH and CLIMB; both positive approaches to becoming AI leaders.

REACH

READ & Research Relentlessly - learn something new every day; be curious & align yourself with other curious people.

EXPERIMENT - Learn by doing, failing & doing again; experiment to innovate.

ACHIEVE - Drive innovation speed results via equal parts superior people, methodology & technology.

CHAMPION CHANGE - Don't just "accept" the pace of change, champion it.

HELP - share with others so they thrive in disruption.

For business leaders, there are certain techniques that will improve the ramp-up towards an AI accentuated business and culture. Culture change can be difficult in any circumstance. AI to many means job loss. How you address the AI-related culture change can make or break the effort.

CLIMB

CEO & Culture – Are they driving disruption within their strategy, and are employees "bought in"?

LISTEN – The pace is moving so fast, you must actively listen to your experts

IDENTIFY – The dominant business model, and your longstanding beliefs about the model and turn them on their head.

MACHINE & Human Collaboration – early on drive the benefits of the collaboration.

BUILD a business model that is agile, can accelerate, can run.

What are Consulting Clients Looking For?

The consulting world is composed of diverse sizes, and specialties. Large firms like Deloitte, PwC, and EY dominate the global landscape. Mid-size firms typically leverage expertise in niche areas to attract their client base. Small firms, often 1-4 employees including the owner, focus on a few key subject matter areas in their offering. Talent marketplaces engage freelancers, often with a great deal of expertise, in non-permanent, project related demands. Over time those demands change as project themes change.

Business Talent Group (BTG), a talent marketplace, issued their 2019 High End Talent Report, a survey of business leaders to identify what they were looking for in independent consultants. The most in demand projects for independent consultants were:

- 61%   Strategy (marketing, sales, growth, opportunity assessment, and product strategy).

- 22% Operations (businesses processes, product launch planning supply chain).
- 9% Transformation (business intelligence and analytics, IT and tech transformation).
- 4% Organization
- 4% Interim executive

The most in demand skills were:

- Project and program management
- Market landscape
- Growth strategy
- Strategic planning
- Supply chain
- Corporate and business unit strategy
- Product development and launch
- Market access and value
- Innovation strategy

The top industries hiring independent consultants were:

- Life sciences
- Financial services
- Insurance
- Consumer goods
- Industrial goods and services
- Technology

The size of the companies doing the hiring:

- 83% large enterprises
- 17% mid-market and small and medium sized business organizations

With those firms hiring through their strategy/internal consulting groups, marketing teams, operations, corporate development, and Profit & Loss owners.

Many more Fortune 1000 companies are turning to independent consultants to meet their project needs, especially during the tight labour market currently being experienced in North America at present.

On a smaller scale, I talk to budding entrepreneurs and tech startups all the time, who have an exciting app concept. Do you know that over 1,300 apps a day were created in 2017 on Google Play, and most apps get fewer than 1,000 downloads? Creators and developers fall in love with their technology, and don't spend enough time with the customer ensuring its solving a big problem in a very simple way. As a consultant you could help them with this very traditional business problem, way back at the planning stage.

What does it mean if as a consultant, you're not getting ready for AI?

- What if your client is running down the AI road and you aren't prepared?
- When your client asks if a native or a hybrid solution is appropriate?

- Are you offering examples of differing predictions for the same time periods, investments, products, etc.?
- Can you use Google search until natural language generation capabilities are available?
- Can you leverage online learning vs traditional learning?
- Can you leverage local sources for information, references, trends?

Ensuring you are considering where the business is, who to speak to, and having a unique offering, increasingly include AI services, can differentiate your consulting firm from others in the same space.

6

Optimum Speed

I retired (for the first time) in 2017. In my early fifties, I discovered the joy of afternoon naps. Wonderfully refreshing! It was during those naps that it occurred to me I had spent the last 25 years making the organizations I led, or was part of, faster. Not the "slide down the hill, out of control on your toboggan" faster. Optimally faster. Faster with risk protection. Our business units began leveraging something we named "optimum speed" to be the disruptor.

By interviewing hundreds of executives, project managers, business leads, and IT experts, I developed the Optimum Speed methodology. My doctoral work focused on innovation speed, in particular how much it actually contributes to business success. My work with MIT advanced my knowledge of AI strategy and in this book you will observe how combining AI and Optimum Speed can be a revolutionary combination in differentiating your business.

Have you ever asked yourself "why can't I get things done more quickly?" What gets in the way. Usually it's some combination of people, environment/structure, leadership, technology, or a lack of information or process that create barriers to speed.

The speed of business continues to accelerate daily. Competitors are finding new ways to accelerate speed to delivery, speed to revenue, speed to market and more. Through numerous interviews and personal experience, I have developed a methodology that teaches you how to accelerate yourself, or your business...through Optimum Speed.

Optimum Speed is an approach to learning, prioritizing, applying, and testing every dimension of speed. Optimum Speed can be applied equally to yourself, your team, and your business unit pursuits. But you have to remember one thing. You are less likely to achieve optimal speed unless you apply all dimensions. Your immediate goal, for example, may be to stop spending Sundays at the office, but you should think more broadly. How can you be a better leader and contributor by accelerating everything you, your team and your business does? It starts with 'are you willing, no..., are you committed to getting faster', and then teaching others?

Let's start with why speed is so critical. Speed provides a competitive advantage - you get to the marketplace and your customers sooner, reducing the time to revenue, and addressing from a position of strength addressing the challenges of competition. From a regulatory perspective, speed contributes to greater efficiency in time spent on achieving regulatory requirements and getting on with our core businesses. From a risk point of view, speed used rationally, can accelerate our prevention and detection of potential or real problems thereby mitigating our risk. From a policy point of view, speed enablers can reduce the time it takes to generate new policies, allowing us to get our products into the marketplace faster. Several studies align with our experience where if we can get to market earlier there is less initial competition, more time to gain market share, an extended sales life, and more. Again, speed to market, speed to value, speed to delivery, speed to revenue. From all of these differing perspectives, speed enables us to achieve our business, individual and team goals.

Many firms establish a vision, mission, goals, and a set of strategies to achieve their goals. The strongest companies are transparent about those goals, and while they're flexible to adapt to changes, they don't pivot erratically or unnecessarily. Peter Drucker, the business guru, once said "There is nothing so useless as doing efficiently that which should not be done at all". So, speed is not the only objective; rather it has to support our prioritized goals. The best business leaders make decisions quickly and execute those decisions faster than others. They believe that fast decisions are far better than slow ones and profoundly better than no decisions at all. They don't strive to be the fastest organization but do value speed as an enabler to those goals.

Speed in a scientific sense refers to the time it takes to cover a certain distance. In a business sense, speed refers to many different metrics. How quickly we get to market with new products, how long it takes to satisfy a customers' need or transaction, how long it takes to devise a new policy, or how long it takes to develop a project business case, are all measures of speed relevant to firms reaching their goals.

While many firms have been around for decades, every year the competitive pace increases and demands they find new ways to be more agile. Competitors, in the past, can consistently get to market ahead of others and the reasons can be numerous. It can take twice as long to develop in-house software applications or tie in off-the-shelf options. Employees often tell employers how "busy" they were but productivity lags the competition. Making a decision can mean extensive research, committees, and layers of approval before being able to execute (see Chapter 15 regarding the buying process). Project managers could describe everything that was wrong with a methodology but may not be able to remove themselves from singular goals like achieving a date, rather than focusing on the objective of the project…to satisfy the customer's needs. Innovative thinkers in the organization can be frustrated when their ideas are buried in favor of the accepted status quo for fear of failure, deciding to merely tweak for efficiency.

Global leaders look outside the organization, and often outside the country of origin to witness some incredible examples of speed innovation. When questioning those owners on the rationale behind the success, the same answers keep coming up. There's no silver bullet. No single tactic or strategy. Such companies look at speed differently, and across the whole value chain. Holistic speed thought, partner relationships, and employee engagement are just some of the ways these companies are accelerating their organizations. Yet great leaders come to understand these ideas, knowing they could not change the culture of their organization overnight. Certainly not by communicating an edict. They need champions in each area of the business, and partners outside along the value chain to bring the ideas to bear and make Optimum Speed sustainable.

Speed is not an individual pursuit. It takes many to teach, collaborate, and implement speed, so speed partners are essential. Leaders don't want employees to just be fast, simply careening down the hill regardless of the cost. They want accuracy & effectiveness. They need to measure and reward speed in terms of the time it takes for the business to realize the expected business value and not in terms of the project start and completion dates. Similarly, they don't want employees to refer to themselves as "busy". Leaders want them to be productive, focused on the companies' objectives, and how all tactics can be used to achieve those objectives, while managing quality, risk, and cost.

Whenever one thinks about speed, don't get caught up in the terminology of acceleration, velocity, agility, etc. In the last decade, more and more people have been talking about 'agile' which, on its own, is important but when you think of true speed, it's more important to think about all dimensions of speed; that's Optimum Speed.

A few years ago, I read a book by change guru John Kotter called 'A Sense of Urgency' and it really spoke to me. I realized that I, and my team, had fallen into complacency, and needed to jumpstart our everyday. That book really brought urgency and its benefits into focus for us. So now I think about Optimum Speed in terms of urgency.

In leading operations support teams in the past, I've watched different people in the operations environment and realized early on that not everyone was created equal. Many of them do the same jobs, but some do more than others do in a given day. When I asked supervisors and managers about this, they responded that the fastest is not always the best. Some place less emphasis on quality, and often have to re-do the task, rather than getting it right the first time. They consistently commented that the best employees combine speed with quality.

For leaders of Community Relations teams or CR, you might not think that speed would be important. But you couldn't be more wrong. When the firm has a problem that becomes public through social media for example, the response team has to be fast, professional and effective. It's important to think about speed from a variety of perspectives. The CR employees reduce reaction time by having clear lines of sight to the right information, the right people, the right external connections so that they can compile a media message with a sense of urgency.

While we've come up with a definition of Optimum Speed, firms may characterize it differently. Optimum Speed, to us, is the best possible rate at which someone or something is able to move or operate given the most favourable conditions. We choose to consider those conditions in six unique categories, to help us achieve Optimum Speed namely culture, organization, methodology, process, technology, and behaviour.

Optimum Speed Methodology
Culture

Optimum speed culture includes integrating or actioning leadership messaging, measuring the competition, creating and leveraging speed communities, and rewarding speed. Culture refers to the distinct ways that people, who live differently, classified and represented their experiences, and acted creatively. It also refers to an integrated system of learned behavior patterns which are characteristic of the members of a society and which are not a result of biological inheritance. So that's the technical view but what it means for you as a business is consistent with that definition.   It's understanding the answers to questions like - What are our executives saying about speed? Are we both internally and externally aware? Do we create and support communities of speed partners? And do we reward and recognize our people for achieving speed? These behaviours demonstrate a company's speed culture.

Here's an example of a speed culture at work. In this case, speed of delivery. Amazon, the electronic commerce company, is currently the largest Internet-based retailer in the world by total sales and market capitalization and no other company has mastered fulfillment quite like Amazon. Speed is a real priority. Amazon knows that customers appreciate the instant gratification of a retail store purchase, and since they offer only online buying, they want to provide the next best experience with all of the cost, and convenience benefits of online shopping. Amazon Prime - the company's paid membership service - guarantees two-day shipping (in some locations same day) on all products in the Prime category. When customers try Amazon Prime they often don't want to return to regular shipping and are willing to pay for the faster service. Amazon's investment in an infrastructure of robotic/automated warehouses support that speed culture. Amazon Prime continues to grow as a service offering, and as part of Amazon's speed culture, because customers want the faster service.

Organization

Optimum speed organizations include reduced bureaucracy, a lean structure, speed measurement, and best practice interaction with other Lines of Business (LOB's). Companies in the mature stage of development are often characterized as stable, and highly profitable. Then competition happens. Often from the most unlikely of places. The firm can be unprepared to make big changes like a large cargo ship in a small port trying to turn around. What's needed is to be nimble to adapt to change and frequently mature companies are not. Fortunately, some are able to react in time, saving key markets and customers by adopting a leaner structure with fewer layers to the decision-maker, by reducing the amount of approval levels within the bureaucracy, and by having each business introduce speed measures to stay focused on being nimble. Finally, getting each line of business to open up the lines of communication to share best practices, synergies, and projects enhances an organizations speed.

The effort is worth every calorie. This type of thinking does not need to just be at the top of the organization. Within your team do you have any bureaucracy, structure, or metrics challenges?

If you use these ideas of creating organizational speed, you, your team, and your business have the potential to move faster. Don't forget though, there was a reason to put the bureaucracy, and structure together in the first place. But they don't have to be conflicting ideas. Sometimes bureaucracy and structure just evolve without a clear, consistent retroactive review. So, go back and look at whether your firm is optimized and nimble for change.

Here are the questions, you should ask ourselves about organization.

- Have we reduced our bureaucracy?
- Do we have lean structures throughout and across our businesses?
- Are our speed measurements consistently applied, analysed, and executed on?
- Do we have the best proactive interaction between LOB's?

There are people within your organization dedicated to making things faster, and they are in every business, and every function. They have the ability to balance speed with those other critical factors like cost, risk, and quality. When you begin to think about how you can accelerate you, your team or your business, leaders should try to connect with them to safely do so.

Speed is a way of thinking. At the macro level, there are some organizations who are thinking about speed differently than they did before. In the US healthcare industry, groups like the Academy for Healthcare Infrastructure are changing the speed to market question from "How quickly can a project be designed and constructed?" to, "How quickly can healthcare and services be provided?" They recognized the short and long-term importance for their organization of speed in each of the cultures of their healthcare partner organizations, but speed for customer value's sake.

Technology

Optimum speed technology includes standardization in technology, minimized customization, shorter deliverable periods, and prioritization of technology projects. When the competitive environment is changing so quickly, and new ways of developing and applying technology evolve, companies have to be collectively fast. It's not a choice, its survival. Do you remember how people started putting GPS units in their cars? Over a period of just 18 months, GPS manufacturers lost 85% of their market value, because smartphones started to integrate GPS technology, for effectively no cost. Tough to compete against that kind of offering isn't it. It all changed so quickly!

For all companies, this should be a wake-up call recognizing the need for speed and a roadmap to get there. Where the magic comes is in applying the six dimensions in the context of managing cost, risk, and quality as well.

For technology alone, companies need to constantly monitor developments in the field because it is changing so quickly with AI, cloud environments, API, apps, mobile devices, and so much more. We often talk about agile, but that's just one approach to technology under certain conditions. Firms need to be nimble, maintain a sense of urgency, and produce in shorter deliverable periods.

Here are the questions we asked ourselves about technology. We continue to ask ourselves these questions to see if we have progressed.

- Have we made progress in standardization of technology?
- Have we minimized customization and favoured configuration?
- Have we managed shorter deliverable periods?
- Have we managed to appropriately prioritize among technology projects?

Methodology

Optimum speed methodology includes active and consistent review and execution of lessons learned, reviewing the gating process in methodologies, the ability to review multiple options, clearly defined scope, and experimentation/fail fast. Project Management Methodology, Systems Design Life Cycle, and Lean & Six Sigma Methodology are crucial to success and practitioners of these methodologies exist throughout organizations. Each of these practitioners follow these methodologies because they are globally developed, accredited, and governed. As leaders, we count on each of them to follow these steps to contain risk, and manage within scope, cost and timing. They protect the firm's interest.

But that does not mean they can't work together to accelerate. They count on each other to coordinate activities, reduce or eliminate duplication, use the right artifacts or documents, and to focus on the objective, understanding that competition is forever knocking on the customer's doors.

At a certain stage, organizations become pretty mature at those respective methodologies. They have experienced and trained staff. Business partners value their expertise. Yet if projects, large and small, are taking the same amount of time as they had the previous year on average, the organization will fall behind. So, it's critical to bring together the various functions, and map out the various methodologies to identify synergies, duplications, and the ways the company operates. Also looking at the planning process before these functions are even engaged can recommend new methods to gain better clarity at the outset.

Outlining options at every stage before making a decision on how to proceed is also critical. This approach is worth it because companies now get more projects done in less time. For every plan or action item coming out of meetings, a due date is assigned and then for items on the critical path the question is "Why can't this be done sooner?" Google's Larry Page was known for asking "Why not? Why can't we do it faster than this?" and then waited for people's reaction, believing that fast decisions, unless they're fatal, are always better. When you apply this thinking consistently the people become very creative in their thought process to speed up the organization.

IT is a critical partner in the speed journey and have an equally important role to play. While IT won't eliminate steps that protect the firm and customer, they can recognize there are new ways of developing technology every day, and that speed partners are trying to achieve the same goals. By aligning IT methodology with project and process, and getting higher quality requirements from business partners, companies can reduce the overall time to implement projects. By also actively looking at lessons learned from relevant projects, companies limit making the same mistakes, rather leveraging the best of what worked in the past.

Here are the questions companies can ask themselves consistently in the methodology dimension:

- Are we engaging in review and execution of lessons learned?
- Have we been successful in reviewing the gating process in methodologies prior to starting?
- Do our teams leverage the ability to review multiple options?
- Do we insist on, and achieve a clearly defined scope?

As a consultant to the functional groups, you rely on their expertise, and at the same time, apply pressure to accelerate, knowing leaders have the same pressures from customers, and competitors. Alignment on speed is critical, and it's important they all embrace the idea.

Process

Optimum speed information includes speed process comparison, an end-to-end view, leveraging synergies, and leveraging business intelligence.

Most companies state these days that "The customer is at the center of everything we do." So, companies need to keep this perspective in mind as they design new processes. The customer thinks about a need they have to fulfill, and from that point to where their need is fulfilled (hopefully by your firm), and you need to offer them seamless, rapid, quality interactions. They care little about what goes on behind the scenes if the process is truly seamless, rapid, and accurate, meeting and exceeding their expectations. So, you need to make the process as efficient as possible internally to keep customers coming back. It's all about a complete customer journey.

If your company is to be truly legendary, from a process perspective, you need to create simple processes that permit quick solutions to problems whenever they arise. The customer has so many choices these days. Competitors are not the same as a decade, or even a year ago. They keep changing and emerging.

In designing new processes, reach out to front line people for input, talk to customers, and have coffee with colleagues. All of these interactions will continuously improve the overall process design.

These are questions companies should ask themselves about their speed process.

- What have we concluded from speed process comparisons?
- Do we continue to leverage End-to-end views, and what improvements have resulted?
- Have we been leveraging synergies in our processes?
- Are we becoming more expert in handling Data & Business Intelligence (BI)?

Bringing teams together, firms can hope that people broaden their thinking about process and see ways they can accelerate what they do in process design, partner collaboration, and weighing the elements of risk, cost, and quality against speed. Getting people to think differently. More holistically. Those other factors should not be considered barriers to speed. Effective people have a sense of urgency, and ensure they include an assessment of risk, cost, and quality in everything they do. When groups design processes they need to consider how the customer would want the process to work, quickly, accurately, and at a reasonable cost. One example is from the Dr. Pepper Snapple (DPS) Group in Plano, Texas. DPS says they want to be the best beverage business in the Americas. They have elevated process improvement to one of their top three strategies through their Rapid Continuous Improvement program - change that is rapid, breakthrough and employee-led. In 2011, DPS adopted Rapid Continuous Improvement ("RCI"), which uses Lean and Six Sigma methods to deliver customer value and improve productivity. As of 2015, the company's RCI productivity program had helped in achieving over $200 million in annualized cash productivity, increasing warehouse efficiencies through optimal use of warehouse space and by reducing driver check-in and check-out times by 50%, and by eliminating more than 250,000 annual transportation miles by shipping direct to customers. That's process improvement contributing to Optimum Speed.

Behavioural

Let me offer one example about the behavioural dimension from over 50 years ago. It's all about the concept of 'failing fast'. Thomas J. Watson of IBM said "Would you like me to give you a formula for success? It's quite simple, really. Double your rate of failure. You may be thinking of failure as the enemy of success. But it isn't at all. You can be discouraged by failure or you can learn from it, so go ahead and make mistakes. Make all you can. Because remember that's where you will find success."

Very few organizations live these principles for fear of taking on too much risk, yet many of the best innovators and inventors have used the education from failure to improve the speed of their businesses. Bill Gates has always said he learned much more from failure than success. Failing fast, learning and trying again is a behaviour that is not common but is necessary for success. So here are the behavioural questions we ask:

- Do we have clear, efficient interaction models?
- Have we embedded clear decision rights?
- Are we actively closing talent gaps?
- Have we developed and executed on speed training for our teams?

How you work, how you interact with others, how you all make decisions, where and how you get trained, where the gaps in knowledge and overall firm talent are...those are all part of our behavioural dimension of speed.

Individuals & Teams

Employees used to tell me things like "I get a lot done first thing in the morning before others arrive", "I take way more brief breaks in the afternoon as I feel more tired then", "I'm sometimes double and triple-booked for meetings", "I have blocks of time where I don't move away from my desk", and "I spend most of my time outside of meetings working on my reports but I can't seem to get them done." When I asked questions like why don't you have time during the week to get your reports done?, where is time wasted?, how do you prioritize your work with your manager?, what inputs are you dependent upon for your reports that might slow you down?, which meetings are ineffective or are too long?, which ones neglect summary notes right afterwards? and which ones don't have a decision made?, the responses varied.

The purpose of a daily personal log is to bring these things to the surface, find out where time is wasted, when you're most productive, and areas you need to improve. Work on what you can control first, get back some of your time, and then look at the next level...teams.

Teams need clear, efficient interaction models. They need to know who is accountable for what and have clear concise communication to reduce what I call 'loopbacks'. Teams need to know who can make which decisions and those decision-makers need to be present.

At the line of business and firm level, leaders need to be assessing any speed talent gaps. If they have speed partners who can do the job, then support them. If they need additional speed talent, then look outside the firm for experienced, successful speed practitioners. Thus, the evolution from individual behaviour to organizational behaviour? Without the right people the firm can't be successful despite all the process, methodology, technology, culture, and organization. That's why Optimum Speed uses all six dimensions holistically. They are interrelated but it all starts with having the right people.

The People Side of AI

"The key to successfully navigating the Fourth Industrial Revolution is more than simply learning new skills. It is knowing yourself and the unique value you have to offer any potential customer or employer." Larry Boyer, Author of "The Robot in The Next Cubicle".

What Employees Want Today

In the past, employees were motivated by pensions and relationships with their manager. Their needs were their paycheck, 9-5 hours, an office to call their own, and a career with the same organization. Todays employees are different. They are motivated by purpose and meaning, they need to make an impact (and of course, get paid); they will work "whenever", and "wherever" suggesting they are more comfortable with flex hours and flex places including working remotely. **Michelle Moore is SVP, Global Product Development at LHH Knightsbridge. She is an expert on the human resource impact of innovation.** Michelle says "millennials are interested in purpose rather than loyalty, they want a career path, they want to get ahead faster, more projects than roles (internal gig economy)." For Michelle, the question she is asked most often when she leads presentations is "how can I make disruptive talent work within a traditional organization?"

Workers aren't leaving...

In the decade from 1900 – 1910, the rate of job churn was 30%. At least a third of employees were changing employers. Over the next 100 years the rate of churn fluctuated between 20 and 35%. Yet in the period from 2010 – 2015, the rate of churn fell to just 6%. If automation were throwing masses of people out of work you'd see lots of churn from job to job. Yet the rate is at an historic low. Workers are staying put, and the issue of robots may have something to do with it.

The very nature of human roles will change because of those robots, becoming more specialized and focused on insights, creativity, emotion, judgment and purpose. Edwin Suarez, the HR director I introduced you to earlier, states "Once commitment is mobilized, you should worry about talent. You don't want to compete for talent unless you are ready and serious about undertaking a transformation." Given the price level of scarce global AI talent, I couldn't agree more. He continues, "Not only is it difficult to find available good talent but once you find it, you don't want it to leave because the intention to transform is just that. When the culture of the organization is not aligned to build

107

the new capabilities that come with a digital transformation, the people with the ability to build it will go. It will also hurt your image and reputation in the talent market."

As a business leader or consultant, you must be constantly looking internally, and be aware of and support the most innovative employees. Why? As Gijs Van Wulfen, a globally respected innovation guru, says "Organizations frustrate their most innovative employees". So, how about changing the roles within your organization to align your needs with employee skills. It's past time to understand the changing job titles, roles and tasks within roles in Industry 4.0. Now, let's take a look at that future and what new roles now exist in the marketplace.

New Jobs That Didn't Exist 10 Years Ago

Job titles – how many have you had in your career? At last count it was 23 for me including "author". Job titles change based on numerous factors and the same phenomenon is certain to appear in the future. For example, the following is a list of job titles that did not exist in 2008.

- App Developer
- Millennial Generational Expert
- User Experience Designer

- Chief Listening Officer
- Sustainability Expert
- Eldercare Expert
- Cloud Computing Services
- Social Media Manager
- Market Research Data Miner
- Data Scientist
- Data Architect
- Data Visualizer
- Data Engineer/Operator

So, when you are looking to populate your organization, consider two forms of alignment: 1) align the tasks or jobs you need done with the types of roles that will exist into the future, and 2) align the tasks with the type of people who are flexible enough to adapt to not only your existing requirements but also the evolution of their roles, perhaps even in ways neither you nor they can yet perceive.

Reskilling

According to PwC's 22nd Annual Global CEO Survey, 55% of CEO's are 'extremely concerned about the availability of key skills and that talent are able to innovate effectively (this is where you as a consultant may find opportunities!). Further, global chief executives believe AI will change the world, but so far many are not capitalizing on it. When asked about "what impact does availability of key skills" have on your organization's growth prospects, those responding 'extremely likely' were clear on their concerns, which are listed below::

The firm is unable to innovate effectively – 55%; people costs are rising more than expected – 52%, quality standards and customer experience are impacted – 47%; the firm is unable to pursue a market opportunity or cancelled or delayed a strategic initiative – 44%, missing growth targets – 44%; only 4% said there is no impact on the organization's growth and profitability.

Will traditional methods of re-skilling work effectively in 2020 and beyond?

Did you know, the four-year degree programs offered by large academic institutions, with their high fees run the risk of becoming outdated? Will non-traditional methods prevail with nano-degrees and certifications at lower or no cost (think Coursera, EdX or Udemy) that substantially shorter time to complete (i.e. two weeks to six months) and feature course materials which are constantly being updated online (think MIT Executive programs). Consultants need to balance the human aspects of what they do, the EQ, with the automation they can leverage. Small Business owners should be looking at their goals and align what's becoming available with reskilling themselves and/or their valued employees

If you are leading or planning for learning and development (L&D) activities within the organization, are you aware of the top priorities in other organizations? LinkedIn Learning's 2018 Workplace Learning Report provides some clarity on the top priorities for your L&D programs:

- How to train for soft skills.
- Consistent valuable global training.
- Delivering insights on internal skills gaps.
- How to track skill development.
- How to access skill competencies.
- Understanding the impact of technology.

Training for soft skills (leadership, communication, collaboration) rather than technical or role specific skills is the top priority for talent developers. If you are part of the HR world, then are you aware of the top challenges for talent developers (in order) according to LinkedIn Learning? They are listed below:

- Getting the employees to make time.
- Getting managers involved.
- Limited budget.

- Demonstrating ROI.
- Employee growth mindset.
- The challenges of a small L&D team.
- Aligning to overall strategy.
- Lack of data & insights.

Finally, as you consider the variety of approaches to learning in the AI environment, employees need to truly become lifelong learners given the speed of changing skills requirements. How can this be accomplished? Giving employees experiential learning opportunities, supporting internal start-ups, integrating ideas from other industries, and brief but thorough industry appropriate programs. As the shelf life of skills shrinks, business leaders worry that talent developers are focused on training for today's skill demands, at the expense of preventing tomorrow's skill gaps. Talent developers are depending more on online learning solutions to meet the needs of an increasingly diverse, multi-generational workforce—and there's no turning back. If employees can't find the time to learn, reduce the friction. Meet them on platforms they're already using with messages that align to their on-the-job needs and professional aspirations. Online learning is critical to lifelong learning in 2019 given its ability to provide training where you want, when you want, and how you want, in particular, learning where your employees meet online.

Role Groupings

One way to think of grouping human jobs related to AI going forward is Accenture reference to the model of trainers, explainers and sustainers. The first group, trainers, are those roles that train AI systems in a variety of ways, reducing or eliminating bias, integrating cultural perspectives, detecting sarcasm, and increasing accuracy and fairness while meeting the objectives of the business.

Explainers focus on the black box challenge with AI. Their ability to understand what really goes into an algorithm coupled with an ability to succinctly explain it to management teams, is powerful. Experienced explainers maintain inventories of algorithms, their uses and explanations, and help management in selecting which algorithms to use in the AI system.

Sustainers are those roles that continuously assess the cost of AI systems and their performance. They elevate or demotes algorithms based on that performance.

I added one more role to this dynamic – that of 'Gainers'. Those benefitting from AI have a responsibility to understand in as great detail as is practical not only the roles of the trainers, explainers and sustainers, but how they align to the goals of the organization, and other strategies being applied to those goals.

The Adoption Gap

As a consultant in the age of accelerated digital disruption, allocation of time and resources continues to be a problem but at an accelerated rate. While investments in technology can be risky at best. Yet some argue that accelerated technological innovation is not the primary challenge posed by digital disruption. Rather the uneven rates of assimilation of these technologies into different levels of human organization is the biggest issue.

If true, then companies must look at their organization and their management in light of this increasing pace of digital change, beyond technology. For leaders looking at the differences in pace of change between technology, individuals, businesses and public policy, Deloitte's 2017 Human Capital Trends study argues they change in the following order: technology changes faster than individuals can adopt it, individuals adapt more quickly to that change than organizations can, and organizations adjust more quickly than legal and societal institutions can.

If you were one to plot the rate of change of technology, against individuals, against business and then public policy, you would see an exponential increase in each area with distinctively different rates of change starting in the 1970's. Technology is pacing much faster than human development, which is faster than business, and much faster than public policy. HR's opportunity is to help close the gaps among technology, individuals, business, society and governments.

Everywhere we look, there is acceleration of computers in terms of their processing power, wireless capabilities, IoT, and more. And since individuals, businesses, and public policy lag technology acceleration rates, incredible challenges exist in terms of adoption, adaptation, and adjustment. Each of these gaps poses a different challenge for companies with respect to digital disruption. Challenges like adaptation, and adjustment.

Adaptation & Adjustment

I remember back in the late 1990's when employees entering our workforce were doing so with increasing frustration. For the first time, their computers at home were far more powerful, and functional, than their desktop counterparts at work. And when they discovered that they could not use a messenger app at work (their work computers weren't even loaded with messenger software), the frustration doubled. The fundamental gap between how the majority of humans want to use a certain type of technology, and the manner in which companies have adapted to the technology is not always successfully aligned as the above example illustrates.

The way in which companies leverage digital tools and how society restricts or governs that use are not always the same thing. Particularly from a timing perspective, where historically legal institutions have lagged technology development. If you're a business leader whose organization operates in multiple countries, you'll know what I mean. Policies and regulations in those countries likely differ, and thus applying technologies equally can be challenging. Holding data in one country but using it in another for example.

Human & Machine Balance

"I've said that machines don't run businesses, people do" argues Edwin Suarez. "Even if we optimize and automate process to the maximum degree, you will still need humans to make decisions and most decisions are not purely automatic and black and white; the market is sentiment based, isn't it?"

Across industries, according to the World Economic Forum, companies that deconstruct jobs and align work to the most efficient combination of humans and machine create an opportunity for 60-80% more savings than those who do not.

Suarez continues, "We need to start creating the space to think about how AI and automation will change our operating landscape and how that will affect our talent strategy. Reality today is that AI won't be able to replace most jobs, it will be by specific skills and it will take time, it will be gradual. That means we can somewhat plan it and start making decisions preparing for that moment. In my opinion, we have to be more proactive than reactive through systems thinking."

Mr. Suarez goes on to illustrate. "I'll give you an example. I recently started using an AI-powered virtual assistant. It can only book meetings with other people, which I use with external parties (outside of my company). It does the job well enough for me to avoid using a human assistant for that task but it's not capable, at all, to do other activities that an assistant would help you with like buying tickets, organizing content and meetings, updating PowerPoint slides, submitting travel reports, etc. Now that I know that, I can start planning how much impact this technology will have in terms of human capital and prepare the assistant to do more value-added work. Eventually, if the AI assistant becomes capable of much more tasks that can replace a person, the human assistant would be trained to do a different job. Then I can also then create better headcount plans as the technology becomes ubiquitous." Suarez's argument allies closely with MIT's proposition of an integrated strategy where people plans are aligned closely with technology plans for optimal productivity.

Organization Structure

We pose the question here - are Traditional or Non-Traditional Methods better for AI in this environment? In the past, IT departments owned all the development, the CIO was responsible for the enterprise digital footprint, and large-scale projects received all the focus, which consumed long time frames. To compete with smaller, more agile organizations (think Fintech), the business must drive the agenda, the Chief Digital Officer (or whatever creative title is assigned) must have a broader role, and a seat at the CEO table, driving projects lasting 6 months or less. Lastly, and possibly most revolutionary - more coders could reside within or closer to the business. You may have heard the phrase 'Coding is the new Typing'. Well Millennials and Gen Z come hard-wired for coding, and speed. They expect to move fast and get frustrated when it doesn't happen. Certainly a non-traditional approach.

Robots Are Coming...To Take Your Job

How many predictions have you read that robots are coming to take all the human jobs? I restrain myself from making predictions since there are so many pundits out there making their own. Scott Santens published an article in the Boston Globe entitled "Robots Will Take Your Job" not to mention the jobs they have already taken (recall my example of robots in the Chinese factory). Santens argues that every task will be cheaper, faster, more accurately done by a robot in future.

Statistics back up the assertion to some degree. Job disappearance is a reality, at least between 2000 and 2009 where in the U.S. 6 million manufacturing jobs evaporated. Was that change due to the introduction of the industrial robot? Yes, but only in part. During this period, China began its advance in industrial production when it became part of the World Trade Organization. That advance resulted in an new industrial machine producing vast quantities of goods intended for global destinations, outside of the robot impact.

Some believe that the impact of machine learning, AI, autonomous cars, online real estate, etc. has yet to be felt. MIT and other sources believe that jobs will change, on the whole, rather than merely disappear. As of 2017, there were more jobs, and a higher percentage of people employed than in 1890. As you think about the impact of AI within your organization or that of your client, a positive emphasis would be on what skills you require of your employees in the future and start re-skilling them for that need.

How Can Your Clients Leverage AI?

As an organizational leader, assuming you have bought into the benefits and understand the risks of AI (covered later in this book), and you also know that your competitors are running down this road, how can you drive your organizations AI strategy? With your leadership team, you'll need to develop a roadmap for AI, starting small but thinking big with incremental benefits from business and digital transformation. You'll need to build capability in your team to be the go-to-resource for AI thereby stopping business decision-makers from going elsewhere.

Within the organization, take an end-to-end "look-across processes" view to ensure alignment with strategy, risk tolerances, and unintended consequences. Initiate conversations about legal, regulatory and ethical issues at the board level. Escalate the importance of leveraging vendors and ensure the strategic sourcing process does not bog you down. Embed yourself and your leadership team in innovation discussions at summits, conferences, and with centers of innovation.

Over the longer term, a task-based view of work will be needed to make the best use of AI. This will allow you to understand which tasks should be automated and which ones are better suited for people to do. New jobs will be created that are still unimagined.

Institutions and society (the education system in particular) have a role to play in unlocking the full potential of both people and machines in the future. When there's no one source of the truth for innovation, disruption, or AI for example, how do you sift through all of the available information & knowledge to learn what you need to be successful, especially when things are changing so fast? Boston Consulting Group's practitioner framework for AI includes data (structured data, text, speech, optical patterns and objects), machine vision or detecting faces and objects in images, speech recognition (transforming spoken words into text), and natural language processing (detecting the intent in a text-based command).

BCG suggests that digital transformation is a journey starting with education, moving on to crystallization, then acceleration, and finally the scale up and transformation. The company completes a digital health check and understands digital trends and ecosystems. Then it creates vision, targets and strategy. It then builds new businesses, transforms core offerings and customer engagement, transforms technology and operations, and builds digital capabilities.

Certain functions within a business differ in technical feasibility (or the percentage of time spent on activities that can be automated by adapting currently demonstrated technology). McKinsey & Company determined that managing others and applying expertise is considered the least susceptible. Stakeholder interactions and unpredictable physical work come next. Data collection, data processing and predictable physical work are highly susceptible. So, as you consider approaches to technology, human EQ is still highly relevant and less susceptible to tech, not surprisingly, as compared to the repetitive data driven tasks.

The 2018 BCG & MIT Sloan Management Review survey on the impact of artificial intelligence on business illustrated the effect the adoption of AI would have on an organizations offerings and processes in five years. Logistics, transportation, IT, insurance and consumer topped the list of greatest effect on offerings and greatest effect on processes, while not surprisingly the public sector, agriculture, energy, and construction lagged all other industries.

What about readiness to invest in AI? According to a 2017 Forrester study of business and tech professionals, interest in AI is high, adoption is in the early stages. The various stages highlighted in the survey include interested (15%), evaluating/researching (20%), piloting POC (18%), implementing (7%), Expanding (10%), no plans (23%), not ready to invest in AI (6%). The same study asked about areas of the organization that are "leading or evaluating the investment and adoption in AI systems". There was some overlap as marketing sales (46%), customer support (40%), product management (40%), engineering (31%), CEO/board (25%) represented the top areas.

From RPA to AI

Robotic Process Automation, or RPA, has been around for decades in some form or another, and the premise is simple. Automate tasks that are repetitive and require little in the way of oversight. But each business is different, at least in terms of its stage of maturity. And when considering the levels of automation maturity, each business needs to consider the stage, and types of technology aligned to that stage.

In the basic digitalization stage, where the technology is merely acting and not truly thinking including desktop automation, quality testing and backend interaction where rules are static – consider employing screen scraping and Optical Character Recognition, document workflow, task scheduling, and web and email interaction.

In the enhanced digitization stage, the automation of basic decisions, analyzing unstructured data, naming entity extraction, sentence segmentation, and speech tagging where the rules are static, and there is contextual knowledge – consider applications like natural language processing, content analytics, process automation and enterprise search and insights.

In the final stage, there are cognitive decisions (thinking) within the automation where the technology understands customers, has query rules engines, and completes transactions with dynamic rules capability, extensive knowledge, requiring a real-time data feed. In these cases, consider cognitive computing, data mining and pattern recognition.

While all of that may sound highly technical, think of them as points on a continuum from simple to complex and moving from RPA to AI. Consider the enablers of work automation capabilities like robotic process automation (RPA), cognitive automation (CA) like AI and machine learning, and social robotics (SR). Tasks under these auspices can be routine, or creative, or collaborative and vary in terms of volume. RPA solves for routine, high volume tasks and has been in use for over a decade. As such it is reasonably stable and mature. CA can wrap its virtual arms around non-routine and creative tasks and can make a significant impact within the organization yet is nascent in its development cycle. SR typically incorporates routine, specific tasks, that collaborate with humans.

Where are AI Investments Happening?

Executives in companies around the world are increasingly looking to artificial intelligence to create new sources of business value. This is especially true for leading adopters of AI — those that have invested in AI initiatives and seen impressive results. This small group of companies is doubling down on AI investments, building competencies, and working to take AI to scale.

Which industries have made the leap to AI? In some way all of them, but to varying degrees. BCG & MIT conducted a study in 2017 called "Reshaping Business with Artificial Intelligence", and determined that across industries AI was expected to have a strong impact. Yet the impact varied to the extreme between industries. Agriculture, utilities, the public sector, and construction, all suggested a smaller effect of AI on processes and offerings, in 2017, and relatively in 2022. That was not expected to change, yet they moved from a 5% impact to a 45-55% impact. IT & Tech, Media, consumer, chemicals and retail, all strong AI adopters in 2017, would vault from 20% to 60-75%. The 2018 study by these two groups suggested "The companies that see the potential and opportunities with artificial intelligence are deepening their commitment...they're following a thoughtful strategy, and they're growing their teams to consolidate their leadership in this area."

So as a consultant, you keep hearing the buzz about AI and digital transformation. "They" say it's happening in every industry (although, as mentioned earlier, studies suggest much more so in some than others. For example, compare Financial Services to Construction.

Yet how do you separate the myths from the realities? BCG's Henderson Institute and MIT's Management Review completed a study which served to dispel several major myths about Artificial Intelligence.

Myth #1: the main benefits of AI align to technology players. The reality is that AI is providing true value to those businesses already applying AI.

Myth #2: by increasing the number of pilots, organizations can scale AI more successfully. The reality is successful companies have an AI strategy, and scale their AI solutions.

Myth #3: the primary benefit of AI is cost-saving. The reality is most pioneers expect AI to deliver increases in revenue.

Myth #4: widely available AI tools will level the playing field. The reality is there is a growing gap between pioneers and laggards.

Myth #5: the US is leading in the AI space. The reality is the level of investment and outcomes in China, contributes to Chinese AI pioneers being ahead of the US.

Barriers to Successful AI

We've discussed the wonders of AI and how to consult to clients about the AI opportunity, however like any business problem you've consulted on, there are barriers to implementing AI within any organization. The list can be long...but not insurmountable.

- Attracting, acquiring and developing the right AI talent.
- Competing investment priorities.
- Security concerns resulting from AI adoption – ie Is there a privacy issue?
- Cultural resistance to AI approaches.
- Limited or no general technical capabilities.
- Lack of leadership support for AI initiatives - Unrealistic expectations of AI within the organization or Media propagates myths with superlatives.
- Unclear or no business case for AI applications - can you do it at scale? Is there a social cost? When you operationalize it, what happens to my job?

- Availability of data? Availability of unbiased, accurate data? Availability within data lake?
- Research by telecommunications giant BT and The Economist Intelligence Unit, conducted in September 2017, found that digital transformation tops the boardroom agenda for nearly 40% of CEOs globally.

Unfortunately, however, the vast majority (86%) of CEOs said they are struggling to deliver their digital programs for reasons that include inflexible legacy systems, a lack of relevant technology skills and security concerns. CEO's can address these struggles in a number of ways.

Firstly, they need to change the organizational mindset around digital so that it is no longer a "strategy" and is instead part of standard business operations. Digital should not just be housed in the research and development organization. Every department should continuously innovate using digital as a matter of course. I call this the "stop doing digital and start being digital" approach.

Secondly, they need to collaborate with external partners who can help them make the most of advanced analytics, intelligent automation, blockchain, artificial intelligence, cloud computing and the latest mobile technologies, as well as overcome the hurdles presented by their legacy systems.

Third, they need to have a plan for how they will invest in digital capabilities in the future. What do they need to build themselves and what can they buy?

Finally, true innovation can only happen when new technological expertise is seamlessly combined with more traditional intellectual and manufacturing capital. In other words, organizations need the brilliant minds in every part of their business to connect with one another. They also need to ensure that their recruitment and retention strategies foster diversity of talent and thought.

Software-as-a-Service

Rather than fight the talent war, some companies have elected to pursue software-as-a-service or SaaS. SaaS is a software distribution model in which a third-party provider hosts applications, making them available in a cloud environment over the internet. Examples of SaaS include Google Apps, Dropbox, and Salesforce. As compare to on-premise solutions where all functions are in-house, in the case of SaaS, others manage the following suite of services: Applications, data, runtime, middleware, operating systems, virtualization, servers, storage and networking. It's typically managed from a central location, is hosted on a remote server, is accessible via internet, and users are not accountable for updates to hardware or software.

Advantages to using a SaaS solution include reducing time, money and resources allocated to installing, managing and upgrading software, permitting staff to work on other priorities.

SaaS can be used if you're a start-up or small company intending to launch an online commerce environment, and do not have the resources or time necessary to deal with servers, software, etc. SaaS also works for short-term projects where collaboration is required, and for applications that require web or mobile access including email, calendaring and office tools.

How are Businesses Distinguished?

For every innovation in history, there have been leaders and businesses who leap ahead to adopt it, and those who use a "wait-and-see" approach. Most of my career involved a fast follower approach where we would allow the innovators or pioneers to conduct the tests, fail, and try again until they had a solid product or business model. Today's world of AI is no different, just faster. One recent way to categorize business approaches is by identifying the speed at which companies adopt AI namely as passives, experimenters, investigators and pioneers. Below we describe each category.

Passives, Experimenters, Investigators, Pioneers

We have made the case above that AI is not going away, and notwithstanding the Terminator scenario, there are more positives than negatives. Yet organizations are taking sides. As we discussed, disruption is uncomfortable, and AI is, if nothing else, disruptive. If almost 80% of businesses globally in 2019 are on the side of "wait-and-see", then the other 20% who are embracing the technology have a unique opportunity to leap in front of their competition. Consultants have a unique opportunity to work with companies and leaders in all camps, to improve their competitive positions.

A worldwide survey of over 3,000 company executives by the MIT Sloan Management Review and Boston Consulting Group determined there were four categories in which businesses could be placed. They are pioneers, investigators, experimenters, and passives. Pioneers are organizations that truly understand and have adopted AI. Investigators do understand AI, however they have yet to deploy it. Experimenters are entrepreneurial types who are willing to pilot AI despite a lack of deep understanding. Finally, passives are organizations lacking both understanding and adoption.

The organizations stand in stark contrast to each other. Urgency is a characteristic of the pioneer firm, actively developing AI strategies while less than 40% of passives have the same urgency. For those who have a strategy in place, the contrast is even more vast at 90% for pioneers, and 14% for passives. In fact, several sources argue that by 2030, over 70% of companies will adopt at minimum of one form of AI, so passives will be hard-pressed to remain competitive over the next decade, particularly with those pioneers who have widely adopted AI. As of 2019, PwC determined that 25% of Chinese companies have widely adopted AI, whereas only 5% of U.S. companies have done so, creating a global rift, that may guide how AI evolves.

Organizations that identify the benefits of AI, develop a strategy to integrate AI into their culture and activities, and attract and retain great talent will be the likely winners in the next 10 years. To disrupt industries and transform businesses leaders must both understand the implications of AI and widely adopt the capability based on a long-term vision and plan.

Rainmaker is one of the start-up companies I co-founded in 2018. Its purpose is simple - AI for Sales. But it's not a solution looking for a problem. In fact, based on dozens of customer discovery interviews, we learned that no existing software solution made the task of salesperson input simple. Which meant they were spending over 40% of their time on what they considered administration, and away from the primary function – interacting with the customer. Entering CRM data, scheduling meetings, sending emails, doing customer research, and generating leads, are all functions that AI can perform to give back that 40% of salesperson's time. If Rainmaker does get to market, it will become a "game changing" technology platform for salespeople, consultants, small business owners and consultants to identify, source, connect with and close client contracts. Pioneers who understand the potential of AI solutions like Rainmaker, can transform their own businesses.

9

Data, Data, Data

"Data is the new oil."

"Data is the new water."

"Data is the new electricity."

Each of these phrases has appeared in the media in the last few years. Each to signify the importance of data to humanity. Data feeds artificial intelligence. Without data, AI could not function. So, given all the fuss, what do consultants need to know about data in relation to their own businesses, and those of their clients?

In my final years at TD, our team was one of the leading financial institutions in the pursuit of the application of "big data" to fraud reduction. We brought together large amounts of client data to arrive at a broader view of their activity in order to identify fraudulent transactions reactively, and to leverage predictive analytics to predict where fraud may occur. Machine learning formed part of the toolkit to process these vast stores of data. Bringing data together in different formats from different systems was a challenge, yet the objective was worth the effort. Protecting our customers from fraud.

So, what are some of the benefits of using data in an AI context? Well, one simple guiding principle is the more data you can train AI on the better. AI often uses deep learning and reinforcement learning (rewards) to identify patterns. In general, the broader the data for training the better the results.

In order to consider how data applies to any organization, we will look at the difference between big data and clean data, data labels and classification, errors, data context, and prioritizing data strategies.

So, what's better than big data? Clean data. Which is to say if your databases are made up of data from many years ago, in particular where change is accelerating through all industries, that data may have no relevance. If data is unstructured, unlabeled, and difficult to coordinate, AI may not be able to generate the outcomes you or your client is looking for. It may take too long to "clean" the data to be worthwhile. Many companies begin with clean data projects to derive the kind of insights not only from the data patterns, but from how the company can integrate AI into their business without the complexity of worrying about the "garbage in-garbage out" effect. As well, companies often focus on the most recent data, which is less susceptible to effects that may no longer exist in the marketplace. Prices change, as do yours or your clients' products, services, operations, etc. Data that reflects current realities holds much greater value.

As mentioned earlier in this book, there are several versions of machine learning (ML), including supervised and unsupervised, the distinction being how much labelling exists to teach the artificial intelligence. Some may be familiar with the dog and cat example. If you have thousands of pictures labelled as a dog or a cat, and you feed those into ML, then the ML can run without any human intervention. Alternatively, unsupervised learning does not require labels, yet is much more complex in its implementation. Most companies begin with the low-hanging fruit, namely a supervised learning project focused on clean, labelled data.

Let us, for example, consider Facebook & Google. With millions of tagged (or labelled) pictures of human faces, algorithms could be trained on a massive amount of structured data, (regardless of lighting, angles, etc.) to identify specific human faces. Google users conduct billions of daily searches and thus Google can identify how much time a user is spending on a page, how much time it takes to load a page, and a litany of other factors to determine the optimal options for users.

Another example exists for customer support departments which have "tickets" that are labelled by their issue, like "refund", or "delivery", and the ML automatically records, and adds to its structured database for pattern recognition.

What about errors in either the data or the algorithm? Both are conceivable and happen often enough. Your implementation must allow for some level of error as the ML improves its performance over time. Running ML in the background may be an alternative if the company cannot risk any errors at all as in the case for invoices, or remittance overpayments. In these cases, human oversight continues to be an important component of the AI implementation and operational environment.

Selecting the right environment to perform machine learning is crucial to success. Dr. Ben Waber, PhD, MIT and CEO of Humanyze (an AI-powered people analytics company) says the environment can be "Any business problem where you have hard data, variability, and a large number of examples." Dr. Charles Martin, PhD, University of Chicago and CEO, Calculation Consulting argues "The best problems are those in which there is a very large, historical data set that includes both rich features and some kind of direct feedback that can be used to build and algorithm that can be implemented and tested easily and will either decrease operational costs and /or increase revenue immediately. "

Every AI project should begin with an understanding of the business problem to solve. It should not be a cursory issue. Rather the problem should be a high priority for the business to solve and for the senior leadership to buy into.

Rather than have a solution looking for a problem ("hey doesn't machine learning sound cool!"), consider the priority problems first, then decide if AI in one of its forms is the right tool to solve the problem. As a consultant or business lead, this is the same type of dynamic you deal with every day. Problem first, solution second. AI is no different.

Select a problem that can realistically be solved. If there is little data, or it's completely unstructured, or the data is predominantly outdated, the problem may be a priority, but not easily solved by AI. Consider what is truly mission-critical to the business but is currently unavailable to access. In my former careers, we often commented, "if we only knew", and by that we meant if there was only a pattern in the data (visible to us) that would have provided some incredible insights and changed our approach or conclusions. User or customer behaviour were often prime examples.

When implementing machine learning, it's often easy to get caught up in the miracle of the data analysis, yet without context the output can be meaningless. For example, you ran a campaign for 12 months, and generated new sales, yet the same campaign is not going to be run in the following year. Interpreting results from machine learning require the teams focus on what environment the data was run in, and whether that environment continues to exist in to the period being forecast.

AI and machine learning are all about testing, understanding, tweaking, and testing again. The first run of the algorithm will yield results, though potentially unexpected, or erroneous. Each business case or problem is unique so expecting ML will solve all problems equally is unrealistic. Iterations are typical, and frankly demanded in order to improve the accuracy and return of the ML investment. Machine learning is derived from experimenting, hard thought, complex algorithms, skilled talent, interaction with business experts and clean data. In fact, keep the projects reasonable in size. Dr. Martin argues that you should "Avoid setting up massive infrastructure until you have a handle on what you want to do. You can easily spend 6 months to a year setting up Hadoop and Spark (software) and not see any ROI. Run numerous small samples to ferret out the problems, and then make the samples large enough to be statistically representative".

Machine learning and data analysis are by no means straightforward, yet like the rest of the AI world, can be lucrative and drive competitive capabilities well into the future.

The "Joy" of Failure

Did you Know...

1. 72% of Automation projects fail to deliver benefits.
2. 53% of Executives would not do Automation again.
3. 14% blame poor technology.

Not all is well in the field of AI, and the above statistics, from several sources, broadly intimated, suggest buyer beware. For a field of endeavour that depends upon trial and error and trial again, AI has its share of failures. One of the most notable occurred in 2016. Microsoft developed Tay, an artificially intelligent chatbot. Tay was designed to mimic the language patterns of a 19-year-old American girl, and to learn from interacting with human users of Twitter. The controversy began when the bot learned from the other chatters and started to post inflammatory and offensive tweets through its Twitter account. Microsoft, to its credit, shut down the service just 16 hours after its launch. Microsoft stated trolls had hacked the service. Others contended that the chatters were using such offensive language that Tay used this input to conform to the way chatters normally tweeted. IBM's

Watson had a similar situation when it used profanity after reading entries from the website Urban Dictionary.

Self-driving cars are at the stage where their safety is under question in 2019. Why? The first known death related to an autonomous vehicle occurred in Tempe, Arizona on March 28, 2018. A female pedestrian was killed in the Uber vehicle incident. The car was in autonomous mode and had a safety driver on board, but it still happened because the car, while detecting the pedestrian, decided to not take any action. Don't even get my cyclist friends started on the capabilities of self-driving vehicles!

AI's powerful facial recognition, and graphic illustration capabilities have created a new challenge called deep-fakes. These are realistic images or videos of celebrities superimposed on others. The quality is so good it's almost impossible to distinguish from the real thing. Fake news, fake evidence, and other fakes are eventual developments from this technology.

Are AI systems good at prediction? Unfortunately, not in every instance as evidenced by those used to predict the outcome of World Cup 2018. Companies like Goldman Sachs, German Technische University of Dortmund, Electronic Arts, Perm State National Research University and other institutions leveraged machine learning for these predictions yet most were completely wrong. EA Games however which used sophisticated ML techniques had the best outcomes by not just relying on historical data, but by factoring in player behaviours as well.

Trial & Error

AI competence is only achieved through trial and error – by failing often, learning and recovering to try again. Most mature organizations are less willing to introduce this testing environment given the risk of failure whether internally or in the media. Below are the implications of trial and error for artificial intelligence.

- Risk aversion by leadership to trying.
- Regulatory barriers to trying.
- Sponsorship is important; need to leverage hierarchy.
- Small pilots in large organizations rarely propagate as far as you hope.
- Lack of systemic process that meets needs of the sponsorship.
- Enterprise AI initiatives often fail to deliver on their promise.
- Existing limitations to creating a strong testing environment?
- Scarcity of data scientists.
- Buy-in (starting top-down).
- Dirtiness of data.

- Industry is lacking scalable best practices driving development and management of ML in production.

Learning from Failure

So once technology is in play, does it make sense that the number of humans involved will always decline? Not necessarily.

Look at the case of Cambridge Analytica. Up to 87 million Facebook users had their data/profiles exposed by Cambridge Analytica, a political consulting firm which had worked on the Trump campaign in 2016. Cambridge apparently acquired the data through a Russian-American researcher at Cambridge University, who created a quiz to get data from Facebook users, and while Facebook prohibited the data's sale, Cambridge Analytica allegedly did it anyway. Mark Zuckerberg stepped up quickly to take responsibility, and to fix the issue, yet users continued to question their trust in many applications with their profile data purportedly secure behind firewalls. Facebook made noises about adding back 5,000 jobs in security and community operations, on top of 5,000 added earlier in 2018 and up to 20,000 content reviewers people jobs to augment what the technology will do. There's always a learning process with technology and its usually through failure.

Beyond 2018, many more companies will be reintroducing customer service into the sales channel including adding people as LivePerson has done this year. LivePerson is a publicly held American technology company that develops products for online messaging, marketing, and analytics. LiveEngage is a cloud-based method of customer messaging using Predictive Intelligent Targeting. Businesses can communicate with customers on the web, mobile devices, and social media. LP Insights turns customers' chat transcripts into structured and unstructured data to provide actionable insights.

Mistakes & Missteps

What are the biggest mistakes or missteps that business people make around AI or perhaps another way of saying that might be – what are they missing out on?

1. Trying to do too much. It's good to have big plans over the long term, but critical to focus your efforts in the short term.

2. Missing the boat. The difference with being in the AI world is it goes exponentially faster than anything we've seen in the past – recall the Digital Vortex.

3. Choosing hype over reality – some readers may have heard of the Gartner Hype Cycle. Well AI is a prime example of how technology can be

hyped in the media but does not always live up to that hype. So, it's important to understand what's real, and what's potential.

So, what is the Gartner Hype Cycle?

The concept is to describe the maturity levels of technology over time. Developments are categorized as less than 2 years, 2-5 years, 5-10 years, more than 10 years, and during the cycle stages include 'innovation trigger, peak of inflated expectation, trough of disillusionment, stage of enlightenment, plateau of productivity.

Understanding the maturity stage of technologies important to your business or those of your clients can help drive decision-making.

In the case of AI technologies, most are in the innovation/peak stage and many are headed towards the trough of disillusionment. Over half are not expected to plateau and deliver reliable productivity for mainstream buyers until 2022 or later. While this may appear daunting, 40% offer transformational benefits, and 51% offer high benefits as of July 2018.

The Innovation Cycle

When planning for innovations, organizations need to consider the innovation cycle, and be able to bridge the gap during the period when the euphoria over the innovation has waned and the company is trying to sustain interest internally and externally.

Virtual Operations produces a graphic for the Innovation cycle which emphasizes bridging the gap. Over time strong technology and process excellence teams collaborate on technology solutions driven by clear objectives, a center of excellence, best practice methodologies, and a strong business case. Once the collaboration is in place, successful teams take their experienced capability, and align it with strategic automation, 365 24/7 support and change and project management practices. Sounds challenging to incorporate all of these elements but innovation is challenging. Try, fail, try again. This innovation cycle risk can be minimized by applying each important step.

The CEO/Business Owner in 2020

So how significant is Artificial Intelligence or AI becoming to business? According to Gartner, by 2020, 30% of CIO's will include AI in their top five investment priorities and 30% of new development projects will have AI components delivered by joint teams of data scientists and programmers. By 2025, that number increases to over 50%.

Given the increasing priority, what should organizations and their shareholders expect from their CEO's in this world of AI? Two concepts. Preparedness and realization of value. Yet, the business leaders I've spoken to recently largely feel ill prepared to leverage the value inherent in AI. They don't understand the technology, the potential benefits and risks, the employee implications, and the effect on the company culture, let alone how to execute to gain value from these changes.

Who is at the Center of an AI Strategy?

While some might argue it's the CIO or Chief AI officer (assuming there is one), it's neither. The CEO must be at the center of the AI strategy. Driving discussions on culture, strategies, shareholder and board approvals, investments, talent, and more. If the CEO or Business Owner is pursuing AI as a strategic imperative, they are reducing the overall risks to the organization according to Judson Althoff, EVP of Microsoft's Worldwide Commercial Business.

CEO's are at the heart of every business strategy, and must be there championing AI across the organization, and ensuring employees buy in (which can be a difficult role while employees worry about the future of the jobs). CEO's need to align with IT teams to drive AI into both large and small projects. Based on all the evidence earlier in this book, CEO's that acknowledge the potential of AI and embrace it within their organizations are poised to succeed. Leapfrogging their competitors, transforming their industries.

It all starts with business purpose and key performance indicators. Organizations and their leaders are measured on performance against their alignment with vision, mission, goals, strategies and objectives. Before considering the implications of artificial intelligence, CEO's must review financial, customer, employee, community and operational objectives over various timeframes:

- Financial – growth objectives for revenues, profitability, expense management, regulation.

- Customer – at the center of each decision, without the customer and their clearly identified needs, no business can succeed.

- Employee – satisfaction indices, talent development, ethics. As CEO you must be aware of and support the most innovative employees. Why? As Gijs Van Wulfen, an innovation guru, says "Organizations frustrate their most innovative employees".

- Community – sustainability, charity, engagement – substantial words but so important to your brand and the community you serve.

- Operations – as a former leader of operations teams, I believe their value cannot be overstated. Give them the right combination of leadership, technology, and process, and magic can happen.

At MIT, my cohort of professors and executive peers talked about the immaturity of AI within organizations (outside of large entities like Google and Amazon) but the discussion always followed with the expected exponential trajectory of AI in the next decade. The trajectory impacts both board members and executive alike. MIT Sloan Management review argues "Consider that 50% of the Fortune 500 companies are forecasted to fall off the list within a decade, and that failure rates are high for new product launches, mergers and acquisitions, and even attempts at digital transformation. Responsibility for these failures falls on the shoulders of executives and board members, who concede that they're struggling...The truth is that business has become too complex and is moving too rapidly for boards and CEOs to make good decisions without intelligent systems."

What about investors' expectations? Investors, 67% according to EY's 2017 CEO Imperative Study, actively seek those companies who embed disruptive innovation activities within their overall strategy projects ...even if they're risky and don't provide short term benefits. Those investments are coming in staggering numbers. In fact, IDC estimates that corporate spending on AI hit $12.5 billion in 2017 and will grow to over $77 billion in 2022.

As mentioned above, according to KPMG's 2017 CEO Outlook, most chief executive officers report they are actively working to disrupt their sectors, rather than waiting to be disrupted by the competition. Yet half of CEO's aren't well prepared to gain competitive advantage through disruption according to the KPMG study. The divide between the promise and the actual implementation of AI amongst most organizations remains wide today. In fact, if your organization is implementing AI, it is only 1 in 5 of your peers according to various surveys conducted in the last year. Yet that ratio is expected to increase significantly by 2025.

What are boards of directors expecting from CEO's in the word of AI? Strategic acumen, technical understanding, ability to work across functions, strong entrepreneurial skills and proven partnering capabilities top the list today. Beyond skills, CEO's come with different attitudes about technology. The age of your CEO should be immaterial to their ability to see and execute on the opportunities inherent in the AI space.

While I reviewed some of the following data at the beginning of the book, it bears repeating because even more divisive is the comfort level of CEO's in leading the implementation of AI within their organizations in order to be "AI ready". The multitude of technologies including AI, analytics, cognitive tech, and Internet of Things (IoT) creating interconnected & more informed digital businesses, is referred to as Industry 4.0 by Deloitte Inc. Their 2018 study found that while many are optimistic about its value, just "14% of CXOs (Chief Executive Officers) are highly confident their organizations are ready to fully harness Industry 4.0's changes."

Every industry has pioneers, early adopters, and laggards, yet with the pace of technological change, the gap will expand in the next five years as laggards find it increasingly difficult to keep pace. In fact, PwC's 21st Annual Global CEO Survey found that in 2013 only 11% of CEO's feared losing technological edge due to the speed of technological change, whereas in 2018, 44% of CEO's held that same fear.

It's not simply about knowing what to do with technology, or how fast to do it. For the CEO of 2020, it's also about finding skilled employees and being able to afford their skyrocketing salaries. The 2018 PwC study suggested CEO's were three times more concerned with the availability of such skills in the last five years.

Finding a CEO to lead an organization in the past was based on skills and expertise in functions like leadership, finance, operations, sales, and marketing. The CEO of 2020 must be able to guide their organization through the exponentially rapid acceleration of AI & technological change to remain competitive.

I asked Edwin Suarez if there were any unique issues in the the global or domestic oil markets (ie regulations, GDPR) that CEO's should prioritize in the next 2 years around AI? "I believe the issues are not unique for specific industries, they probably will be more common just different in speed and timing. From my perspective, the number one concern will be about losing jobs so a plan needs to be built, not only to be compliant with regulations, but to retrain and shift priorities while minimizing the impact in employees. The number #2 concern will be around protecting data and data-related intellectual property."

What Should You Expect from the Chief Information Officer?

The CIO is responsible for numerous strategies including leading innovation, monitoring competition, and leading interactions with other functions. Tasks include innovation labs, ecosystems, API Intelligence/prediction, IoT, Cloud, and open source strategy.

CIOs should remind CEOs and CFOs that digital disruption is a fast foe when it strikes, and discuss the full list of ideas with them to see if different or more radical options could be tried. Top performers generate more digital revenue and create more digital processes. They should also:

- be accountable for the maturity level of your digital positioning.
- engage outside the IT department.
- spend more time on executive leadership than IT delivery leadership.
- anticipate the next wave of technology – they are present in the marketplace with technology leaders and understand how to leverage new tech.
- prepare their organization for new technologies.

As you think about the roles that various C-Suite players need to engage in for the AI strategy, consider these activities. For the CEO, mergers and acquisitions, legal action, funding sources, strategies like taking a company private, a spin off and replacing leaders. For the CFO and CHRO consider pricing, revenue recognition, hiring, firing, longer term thinking, cannibalizing products, outsourcing, and investor relations. The Chief Marketing Officer should be responsible for awareness, data analytics, customer service, new targets, media, communications. Sales leaders own channels, contracting, partnerships, direct vs indirect, while product leaders have responsibility for design, features, delivery, patents, microservices, and to some extent pricing. If your organization has a Chief Customer Officer, ensure they are focused on advocacy for customers, value, and communications to customers.

Who Owns the Disruption Program?

In your client organization who truly owns the disruption agenda if they have one? Is it the CEO? How about the Chief Information Officer? Or maybe the Chief Technology Officer? Ownership can depend on the size or stage of the organization. One set of terms used to describe the stage of business are Caterpillars, Chrysalises, and Butterflies. In one report, CEO's were less likely to be the disruption agenda owner in the first two instances (or earlier stage companies) whereas the probability increased substantially if the business was a butterfly.

Funding Digital Transformation

How do organizations pay for their investments in digital transformation including artificial intelligence? Not unlike other investment decisions as it turns out. Corporations use the same investment vehicles as for other assets and software. The interesting part is how frequently each approach is used.

According to a study by Gartner (CEO's and Senior Executives Survey 2017), the top 10 methods of funding digital transformation investments are:

1. Internal Self-Funding (51%).
2. Within Existing Budgets (46%).
3. Investment from Reserves (30%).
4. Increase Relevant Budget & Cut Others (25%).
5. Increase Relevant Budgets and Cut Profits (13%).
6. New Bond/Equity Capital from Investors (12%).
7. Borrow Capital from Lenders (11%).
8. Off-Balance Sheet Entities (11%).
9. Divestitures to Fund (10%).
10. Asset Disposals to Fund (8%).

Most often corporations look internally to fund their investments in digital change. When making investment decisions regarding digital transformation, CEO's should consider Amara's Law which states "We tend to overestimate the effect of a technology in the short run and underestimate the effect in the long run". Developing business cases with hockey stick trajectories or short-term wins is ineffective.

MIT's strategy guru, Professor Donald Sull argues that companies should not look, forecast or project beyond 3-5 years in the future. With the pace of change, and factors outside a companies' control, planning for the medium term consistently provides the most tangible results. Similarly, with investment decisions, 3-5-year time horizons integrating investment, development, implementation, and market adoption should be taken into account. Having said that the traditional 12-18-month IT development horizon is no longer tenable. If the company is entering the market in 3 years, the competition is likely to have usurped the space, and eliminated the opportunity for many others.

Investors in AI

According to data from CB Insights, as of the date of writing, the most active corporate investors in artificial intelligence are:

Intel Capital   Google Ventures   GE Ventures

Samsung Ventures   Bloomberg Beta   In-Q-Tel

Tencent   Nokia Growth Partners   Microsoft Ventures

Qualcomm Ventures   Salesforce Ventures   AXA

Strategic Ventures   New York Life Insurance Company

International Data Corporation (IDC) estimated that global corporate spending on AI would hit $12.5 billion in 2017 and grow to over $77 billion in 2022. In 2017, most of that spending – $9.7 billion – was in the United States, followed by Europe, Middle East, and Africa (EMEA), and then Asia/Pacific (APAC). By 2020, APAC is expected to trail only the United States, fueled by heavy investment in Japan and China.

Part of that spending will be on human capital. In the United States this year, companies will spend over $650 million on salaries for 10,000 jobs related to artificial intelligence, according to a recent study by Paysa. Most of those employees are in well-known technology leaders: Amazon, Google, Microsoft, NVIDIA, and Facebook are the five largest employers of AI workers today.

In 2018, a Gartner CEO survey revealed that CEO priorities were shifting to embrace digital business, and that growth, corporate strategies, IT and workforce issues continue to top CEOs' priorities in 2018. Yet, the survey also discovered that CEO's are looking at the leadership team to assess whether there was sufficient depth in understanding and implementing digital business. Year by year priorities can change. In 2017, the survey concluded that 58% of CEO's stated their biggest priority was growth, by 2018, that number was down to 40%, with the shift focused on strategies of how to grow whether through M&A, partnerships or other strategies.

Before Meeting with The Board

Artificial intelligence creates unique opportunities and challenges for every organization. Boards can explore the potential impact of AI in their company by starting a discussion with senior executives and outside experts around some foundational questions:

- Where are we starting to use – or considering the use of – artificial intelligence in our organization? Are we choosing those parts of the business opportunistically or strategically?
- Who is overseeing the development or adoption of AI in our business? Are they looking at the organization holistically, or are they focused on a narrow part of the company?

- What type of AI expertise do we have on staff? Do they have the skills and experiences that we need? If not, how do we augment that team?

- What are our competitors doing with artificial intelligence? What can we learn from their efforts, and how the market has responded? What are they missing, or where are they stumbling?

- What partnerships can we develop to enhance our understanding of how AI might work in our industry, for our company?

- Are there any legal or regulatory issues that we should take into consideration when adopting AI?

- How should we be addressing AI from a talent perspective? Should we be recruiting a Chief Artificial Intelligence Officer?

At a high level, artificial intelligence is one example among many of how technology and digital capability is transforming organizations. Many businesses will consider this a discipline of digital transformation or data and analytics, and if so, the Chief Digital Officer or Chief Analytics Officer may already be overseeing not only the technology, but the team responsible for it. In a few organizations, this may even be overseen by the Chief Strategy Officer.

Regardless of title, whomever is overseeing AI needs to be able to connect business strategy to emerging AI capability, work cross-functionally, and carefully evaluate whether to build, buy or partner to gain the right AI capability for your organization. When looking at specific candidates, consider assessing them in these areas:

1. **Strategic Acumen**: AI can be leveraged to create disruptive market offerings as well and to fundamentally transform internal operations. Leaders will need to know how to challenge the status quo and push for change, while also being realistic on what the company can do, and how much change it can manage

2. **Technical Understanding**: Data is key to the functioning of AI, so a successful AI leader needs to understand any type of pre-established data strategy at a given company. Additionally, they need in-depth knowledge and currency on the different forms of AI and the impact they can have on the business.

3. **Ability to Work Across Functions**: AI can be applied in myriad ways across a business. It will be important for an AI leader to make sure the technology is evaluated and applied across functions and business lines in synergistic fashion to avoid duplication of effort in multiple siloes.

4. **Strong Entrepreneurial Skills:** AI gives companies the opportunity to create new products and businesses (for example, connected devices), so

a strong leader needs to have an entrepreneurial spirit to help create and guide innovations.

5. **Ecosystem Partnering**: Given the current extreme scarcity of AI technical talent, few companies will be able to hire large AI teams and invest robustly enough to create their own technology from scratch. Whoever oversees AI will therefore need to be able to work with other entities to gain access to the right capability through purchase or partnership.

PwC's 21st Global CEO Survey illustrated the confidence of CEO's in their growth prospects (88%) and clear concern over protectionism in 2018 (84%). In the same study, 68% of CEO's "say AI, robotics and blockchain will disrupt their businesses in the next five years."

The PwC study showed significant differences between countries in their view of the concern over the availability of digital skills in their country. China led others with scores in excess of 92% within their workforce, industry and country where they were based. U.S. CEO's were much more concerned about acquiring that talent within their workforce (86%) versus within the country at only 50%. Canada lagged both at between 60 and 72%

suggesting those CEO's are more confident in Canada's ability to generate that talent or are less aware of the dearth of available talent. The latter may be the case as less than 1/3rd of Canadian CEO's say "they understand how robotics and AI can improve the customer experience. This is significantly short of the 47% of global CEO's". The U.S. was similar at 34%, yet China scored over 80%. What is causing this disparity?

The World Economic Forum believes the issue is an urgent one. In fact, they argue "[A]s the rate of skills change accelerates across both old and new roles in all industries, proactive and innovative skill-building and talent management is an urgent issue. What this requires is a [talent development] function that is rapidly becoming more strategic and has a seat at the table." North American CEO's need to accelerate their understanding of the benefits of AI and robotics, and the need to develop talent to catch up to global competitors like China.

The Mandate for Exponential Leadership

We are living in a "VUCA" world—an increasingly unpredictable and dynamic environment of nonstop Volatility, Uncertainty, Complexity, and Ambiguity. Leading an organization, a business unit, or a team to success in this world, which is not slowing down but rather accelerating, is incredibly hard. Most CEOs today feel a profound sense of urgency to transform everything about their organization (strategy, culture, structure, leadership) to ensure they're able to avoid disruption and thrive in the future.

Transformation starts with people. To be a catalyst for the required change, leaders must first unlearn outdated approaches and legacy behaviors that impede progress. They must embrace a new skillset, toolset and mindset that can inspire and empower both the individual and the organization to adapt and evolve. This is an Exponential Leader.

Many organizations are realizing that their existing leadership development programs are ill-equipped to prepare leaders to meet rapidly evolving business needs. Most programs use outdated methods, set inadequate context, offer insufficient coaching, and are generally too slow to keep pace with changing times. When I was running large teams in the U.S. and Canada, a consistent dynamic was the importance of understanding what was changing, and over time the pace of change continued to accelerate. Keeping teams updated on issues arising within the business meant more people were thinking through the implications of each change. A culture of communication within an environment of acceleration is essential to a business' long-term success. In the era of AI even more so.

If you're a consumer-facing organization that hasn't started a personalization program leveraging AI, you're not alone, but you're also at risk of falling behind. When speaking of exponential change, leveraging big data and AI to integrate personalization into your brand offering, can result in revenue improvements – in fact 2-3 times faster in some studies than those who don't. In fact, it's likely that organizations can capture a disproportionate share of profits leveraging the personalization particularly in retail, financial services and health services.

13

Industry Review – Construction & AI

The need for efficiency is obvious. Especially in the construction industry which has been slow to adopt automation relative to other industries. Cost efficiency, faster completion time, greater accuracy, fewer accidents and injuries, less jobsite theft, are all potential benefits from automation. Yet the construction industry has been slow to integrate automation.

The Economist produced a study in 2017 comparing manufacturing and construction productivity since 1995. Manufacturing productivity doubled that of Construction, and according to McKinsey no industry has done worse during this period. In the U.S., construction productivity has fallen by 50% since 1960.

Here are the traditional key problems with productivity in construction:

1. Only 5% of builders work for construction companies employing over 10,000 workers.
2. Profit margins are lowest except for retailing.
3. Highly cyclical industry including frequent downturns.
4. Investing in capital can be high risk.

5. Lack of skilled employees/contract employees.

The fundamentals of construction have not changed significantly for thousands of years given materials like concrete, timber, glass and bricks are still used and activities on site are often entirely manual, particularly on small projects. Construction is continually criticized for being inefficient, fragmented and slow to innovate, with two-thirds of contractors not innovating at all. Research rarely affects practice.

So, there is a clear opportunity to drive automation into the construction industry to address these traditional problems. As noted above, there may be an expectation from Millennial homeowners for contractors to be adept with automation. Fortunately, technological advancements can provide the answer to efficiency.

This next section focuses on the key advances in construction for the future including smart construction, virtual reality, augmented reality, drones, 3D printing, robotics, remote controlled equipment, building information modelling, e-commerce, and Internet of Things. All are key digital transformation trends that can help potential clients thrive.

Smart Construction

The term 'smart' refers to new, intelligent, integrated, innovative, or improved. In the context of construction, this can refer to smart buildings, smart design and smart cities. Automated buildings with sensors, wireless technologies, and leading environmental technologies are considered smart. Smart design includes enabling a greater perspective on increasingly wide layers of portfolios, neighborhoods, cities, regions, etc. When municipal leaders can integrate physical, human and digital systems into sustainable systems for future prosperity, they are considered smart cities.

Some newly available technologies and workplace practices are expected to enable smart construction going forward should they be successful in being implemented. One example is the adoption of Building Information Modelling (BIM), the promotion of more collaborative working practices, and improvements in off-site manufacturing. Partnerships between government and construction industry partners like the one envisioned by Britain in July 2013, when the Government published: 'Construction 2025, Industrial Strategy: government and industry in partnership'. Britain set out its long-term vision for '…how industry and government will work together to put Britain at the forefront of global construction'. That the industry should be 'smart', '…an industry that is efficient and technologically advanced'.

Construction industry participants in the next decade will need to integrate technological advances, with new capabilities such as the internet of things (IoT). Given the disparity of profit margins, lack of skilled employees (Japan expects to have a deficit of 1 million construction employees in the next decade) and lack of desire to invest in capital, automation is a natural alternative solution to drive step change within the industry. Adding sensors, monitoring, and data management should enable performance increases and efficiency gains in process and asset management. Further, improvements in material usage, scheduling, carbon reduction, and smarter designs are conceivable with automation.

It remains to be seen whether governments and industries in all countries achieve greater collaboration, yet individual participants can take the lead in integrating automation and achieve greater prosperity for their own organizations.

Companies should consider how they can work towards removing barriers to innovation, co-operating in construction innovation research, develop relationships with industry participants and research organizations, sharing innovative ideas, participating in projects that include off-site manufacturing to achieve greater precision and quality and reduced manufacture and assembly time, halving waste and using 25% less energy, and finally enabling their clients to make better use of technology.

Building Information Modeling (BIM)

Public projects have been leveraging Building Information Management or BIM software, which is mandatory for those jobs. BIM platforms/software offer value for a variety of projects including improving communications with clients and other parties involved in projects. Increased transparency and a single source of truth creating a foundation for improved collaboration. Boston Consultancy Group (BCG) predicts that BIM should be advanced enough to deliver productivity gains between 15% and 25% as early as 2025. Use of Building Information Modeling platforms is used extensively in China, is recommended in the EU, and even mandatory for (some) public sector projects in the UK, Norway and South Korea, with Germany to follow in 2020.

VR Aided Design - VR in Home Design

Virtual Reality (VR) became one of the leading trends in 2016, started to dominate in 2017 and will likely continue to proliferate. Real estate agents, designers and people who plan to remodel their houses, apartments or offices are all using VR. VR is being used through 360-degrees image or video of the real house as well as the virtual model of it. Images of the real house can be taken by special 360-degree cameras like Ricoh Theta S, Samsung Gear 360, Nikon KeyMission 360, Kodak Pixpro

4KVR360, 360fly 4K and others. Prices range from $200 to $500, but there are plenty of more expensive solutions on the market. A standard phone camera supporting shooting of 360 degrees images might suffice to do the job. The main disadvantage of 360-degree images is that you are unable to remodel the house you see unless you actually move the furniture or paint the walls.

Virtual modeling software of the design like Live Home 3D can help with this task. Live Home 3D makes panorama 360° images and videos on Mac and Windows platforms to develop creative and advanced home and interior projects. This program helps to design a copy of the house and export the final result into panorama 360° images and videos without need for Virtual Reality headsets as designs created in Live Home 3D can be viewed on any computer or even a mobile phone (2018 BeLight Software Ltd). The market for virtual reality headsets has matured significantly in the last three years. The major players are Oculus Rift, HTC Vive, Microsoft Hololens, Samsung Gear VR, and Google Daydream View.

Internet of Things (IoT)

One way that the construction and building industry can benefit from IoT technology is advanced tracking. For example: wearable smart devices make it easier to track employees. This offers opportunities to improve safety, but also minimize labor waste and even fraud. Another way construction companies can benefit from IoT is equipment and machinery with online capabilities that can monitor and communicate about its own status, streamlining maintenance and repair processes.

Chatbots

ChatBots can offer a pragmatic solution for engineers working in the construction industry, which can be easily integrated into the communication structure they are currently using. ChatBots can manage communication and workflows to increase location-based interaction with equipment and engineers for planning and cost control. Artificial intelligence-based chatbots seem to be one of the most important assistants to construction site engineers. For a site engineer, it is difficult to manage the relationship between design, implementation and equipment usage. Hence, real time support will increase the productivity.

Chatbots offer real time information about machinery and team performance, construction site activity related photo and progress sharing, and tracking real-time activity progress. Similarly, they offer easy access to location related drawings and info, notification for urgent needs and requirements, easy sharing of contractor, warehouse and material info. Furthermore, they can publish daily progress report easily and accurately, notify site engineers, and track real-time activity progress. Finally, chatbots can support "just in time" procurement and contractor management, and much more.

E-Commerce for Materials

With e-commerce for building and construction materials, commercial processes can be improved such as ordering building materials online. The Home Depot's web store offers over 700,000 items online (as opposed to 35,000 products in a typical brick-and-mortar location). W.W. Grainger Inc.'s online sales account for 47% of total sales. Amazon's tools and home improvement sales are outpacing the rest of the market at 35% year-over-year growth. While the total U.S. market was worth $313 billion, it saw just 6% year-over-year growth. Just a fraction of what Amazon realized. Significant demand exists for an easy way to buy tools and materials online.

AR Aided Design

Augmented reality is the incorporation of a computer-generated image on a person's view of the real world. It provides a view of both what the world and work actually look like and what it could look like. Currently, the most popular augmented reality wearable in construction is the Microsoft HoloLens given its price and the fact it's now certified as basic protective eyewear. Users can use computer-generated models both on the site and in the office to see what the final product will look like, proving the value of augmented reality in construction. When clients see computer-generated images or drafts, and they might have a slightly different image or vision from what they expected. By using augmented reality in conjunction with BIM both the architects and construction firms can truly showcase functional models to their clients. Clients can make decisions based on the current plan and make changes before construction starts. By engaging clients early on it prevents costly fixes later and keeps clients interested in the project. They can see their vision, they know they're heard, and they know work is being done. It makes augmented reality in construction a major driver in reducing costs for re-work.

The best benefit to augmented reality is the ability to give project managers the tools to see how everything fits on site before parts are ordered or assembled. Some companies have saved thousands of dollars thanks to errors caught by project managers using a HoloLens. While most companies are using VR helmets, glasses and other wearables on the sidelines for safety, it looks as though it will soon be available to walk through the site. It helps projects managers know how the plumbing, electrical and other utilities will fit into the structure so they can plan for it. Augmented reality is gaining speed in construction as it is one industry that will clearly benefit from it. Construction companies that have implemented augmented reality are already seeing the financial benefits. As the technology gets better, augmented reality will be more common on jobsites and in meeting rooms.

Drone Deployment

According to a 2016 McKinsey report, unmanned aerial vehicles (UAVs), commonly referred to as drones, will dramatically improve the accuracy and speed at which construction projects are completed in the near future. There has been a dramatic decrease in the manufacturing cost of technology and thus the prices of professional grade drones for construction, complete with mountable, lightweight HD cameras and other survey equipment to as little as $700.

Drones alone can dramatically improve surveys, site visibility, progress reporting, and inspection processes. Drone photography can be an important sales tool to win additional business as improved surveying and planning capabilities can set a firm apart from the competition. Drone photography can help owners visualize the final project and see how the project is progressing while under construction. Drone surveys can help put the virtual design in the context of real conditions and thus better engage the entire team. Drones with streaming video capability can help monitor the job site for suspicious activity and identify theft as it's happening. In addition, your teams can easily monitor locations and quantities of assets and materials at a glance, to ensure they will be there when you need them. Drones can improve invoice accuracy as work is monitored to completion more effectively. Drones vastly increase the ability to complete quality inspections in large and hard to reach areas in an efficient manner. Finally, drones can minimize rework via increased inspections to catch more mistakes before they become a bigger problem.

Drones can be used through the entire construction lifecycle, from feasibility and bidding to handover and maintenance. In terms of feasibility, using cameras, geo-location and infrared sensors, data can be imported into software to create 3D models, identifying risk areas, understand constructability, and visualize the end product. During construction, drones can track progress, monitor assets, increase safety, and provide a documentation trail. Thermal leak detection, and other capabilities are valuable in the building maintenance stage.

Robotics

The rise of construction robots comes as the building industry faces a severe decrease in labor supply. One recent study showed that 70 percent of construction businesses have a difficult time finding skilled workers. Robotic technology provides the construction industry with numerous advantages. With the goal of automating processes and increasing productivity, robotics are being used to get work done quicker, cheaper and with more precise detail. Automating processes like welding, material handling, packing, dispensing, cutting and packing through robotics and machinery, allow for precision and accuracy throughout all construction processes, and also represent a significant time and financial savings as well.

Companies like Built Robotics which develops technology to produce self-driving heavy equipment, Construction Robotics whose machine can lay 3,000 bricks in a normal workday (several times more than a human bricklayer can do in the same period, in fact some of the most advanced brick laying machines can complete an entire house within a few days), and drones to measure huge amounts of rock and sand for sale. The machine can measure the materials on the whole 36-hectare place in 25 minutes while the same job takes a human a full work day to do. These are present day examples of robotics opportunities in construction. The policy director for the International Union of Bricklayers and Allied Craftworkers argues his organization supports the rights of construction workers in the United States and Canada and is not worried that machines will replace human workers any time soon.

According to the World Economic Forum, 5 million jobs are expected to be lost by 2020, and 10% of total job losses are forecast to come from construction, where the same amount is due to be needed in architecture and engineering so the needs are shifting with robotics and process automation. Higher quality, accuracy (removing human error) and repeatability are valuable robotic advantages as is speeding up the demolition process (breaking down walls, crushing concrete and gathering all debris) to provide a large saving of time and money.

Eliminating waste (construction creates 20% of the world's landfill) not only improves the environment but profitability. The introduction of 3D printing is continuing to grow in the construction industry. Now it is possible to print complex, layered, parts and objects that can be used in the construction of homes, buildings, bridges and roads. In addition, robotic machines can standardize the production of pieces that can be used throughout various projects, saving both time and money.

Robotic Process Automation

Outside of the physical domain of robotics there is robotic process automation. Companies can, for example, transform their billing operations by automating the activities involved in creating an invoice and its supporting documentation to enhance cashflow. Here's an example from one engineering and construction firm.

"A global engineering and construction firm was experiencing cash flow problems resulting from Days Sales Outstanding (DSO) delays. These delays, in turn, were caused by difficulty in efficiently generating accurate invoices. Each invoice required, on average, more than 150 pages of back-up data that had to be pulled from five-to-ten different systems, including ERP and homegrown legacy platforms, time and expense systems and vendor portals. Compiling supporting documentation for a single invoice required four to five hours of manual effort—and the company was issuing thousands of invoices per month, with a range of different business rules for different business units in multiple geographies. In trying to resolve the problem, the company's IT department confronted technical challenges and resource constraints, while the F&A unit was mired in a lengthy business process reengineering study."

"Advisors from ISG were engaged by the firm's IT department to develop a Robotic Process Automation (RPA) solution to streamline the activities involved in creating an invoice and providing supporting documentation. Working in collaboration with the billing department, advisors began the project by conducting in-depth interviews with process subject matter experts to analyze and document the specific steps involved in creating an invoice. This information was then applied to the next phase of the project, which involved designing how the RPA solution would work. Key issues here included defining how the robots would access systems in terms of triggers and sequencing, how exceptions would be handled and how hand-offs between humans and robots would occur. Subsequently, the RPA software was installed on virtual machines, subjected to rigorous testing and deployed into production. The resulting RPA solution—designed and implemented over the course of eight weeks—has reduced the average time to create an invoice from 4.5 hours to 11 minutes. With a total annual cost of $150K, the digital robots are doing the work of an equivalent of 20 FTEs who were processing the thousands of invoices each month. Staff who remain are now able to focus on managing exceptions and on customer-facing billing activities. In addition to the cost savings, the solution has reduced DSO and accelerated daily cash flow by eight figures."

Conclusion

Now I'm certainly not picking on the construction industry, how it a prime example of an industry ripe for disruption. Construction, as of 2019, evidences a significant lag in technology development and adoption behind other industries. As such, opportunities exist in the near term to derive revenues from packaging/bundling, building, buying and distributing construction technology solutions like the ones described above. Because contracting firms are typically smaller they are less connected and thus integrating automation has not been driven by globally aware senior management. Therein lies an opportunity.

The Board, Regulations and Privacy

The Board

The monthly Board meeting is just a couple of weeks away. Your clients' core business is operating as expected and aligned with your key performance indicator goals. The industry however appears to be not just dynamic but changing at lightning pace. Competitors arise from non-traditional and unexpected origins. The Chief Innovation Officer (CIO) and Chief Technology Officer (CTO) assuming the organization has such roles, are arguing in favour of investments in artificial intelligence. The CEO has a sense that the Board will be unwilling do anything that risks core revenues. The CEO has been considering the opportunities that Artificial Intelligence has brought other businesses in other industries. You have yet to invest yourself, but believe the future is in AI.

So, you suggest what questions the Board may wish to be asking at the next monthly meeting. Do they align with the questions which surfaced during executive leadership meetings in preparation? And finally, what's the leadership teams level of commitment to the AI domain? Those board questions might include:

- How is the management team selecting areas of the company for investment in AI? Is it a strategic rationale or opportunistic one? Is AI part of digital transformation or unique?

- What are our competitors doing in this space, what have they learned and how can we leverage those learnings?

- What are the key metrics being focused on by the management team for the AI investment and how do they align with our existing objectives?

- Do we have a single leader (i.e. a Chief Artificial Intelligence Officer) providing oversight of the development or adoption of AI, and if so are they considering the whole organization or silos of the business?

- In terms of AI expertise, how deep is our internal knowledge and skills versus our reliance on external partners or vendors?

- AI relies on data. Do we have enough accurate, accessible, attributable data to be meaningful, and can be access be controlled in such a way to satisfy our privacy policies?

- When cur employees start to voice their concerns over potential job loss due to AI, have you prepared our organizational culture in advance?

- What regulator or other risks need to be considered with an AI strategy?
- Our brand is very important to our continued success. Can AI augment or negatively impact that brand publicly?

Artificial intelligence provides, for each organization, a set of unique opportunities and challenges. Corporate Boards must acknowledge that technological and digital capabilities are transforming organizations around the globe. Such transformation cannot simply occur at the CIO or CTO level since it affects every aspect of the corporation and its future. Some organizations place this responsibility with the CEO or even a Chief Strategy Officer, yet decision-making for digital transformation must be overseen at the Board level.

Strength in the executive level is a challenge in the current environment given the lack of available AI leader resources. Notwithstanding which title is selected, when considering such roles, careful evaluation of the following AI capabilities is critical.

Inter-function Relationships: In order to avoid duplication or contradiction, look for synergies between lines of business, and ensure technology is being evaluated in a consistent manner

External Partnerships: AI talent is scarce, thus gathering a large team may be impractical. Focusing efforts on multiple solutions will be critical, namely re-skilling employees, relationships with partners or vendors, acquisitions and more.

Strategic Thinking & Business Acumen: Since so few leaders understand AI language, let alone its capabilities, ensuring leaders understand the benefits prior to driving a learning agenda will be crucial to success. Finding leaders who have implemented AI successfully, at present at least, are scarce, and highly sought after, so organizations must select between organic development and acquisition of leadership talent.

Entrepreneurship: Developing new products and services is a natural outcome of AI that identifies new, previously undiscovered patterns in data. Having a leadership that is entrepreneurial will assist in taking advantage of new opportunities.

Privacy

As a former executive in Financial Crimes & Fraud Management at a top 10 North American Bank, I witnessed the effects of hacks, phishing, vishing and smishing (worth a look through Wikipedia) and saw the importance of protecting one's privacy first hand. During that period, in 2015 alone, there were over 175 million records exposed through 780 data security breaches according to ITRC Data Breach Reports, and hacks occurred in every single state in the U.S. In 2017, the U.S.'s biggest consumer cyber-attack was the Equifax data breach affecting over 145 million customers, and overall the number of attacks doubled globally over 2016 affecting billions of internet users around the world.

Still, companies collect and share users' data millions of times every day. They use cookies, web beacons, log files, and other mechanisms to do so. As a user, data privacy is critical to data safety, and fraud protection. Nowhere in the world has this recently become more apparent than in the European Union. The new European Union law (General Data Protection Regulation) was introduced on May 25, 2018, and immediately had effects worldwide in terms of its launch. Organizations on every continent integrated GDPR rules (particularly Article 6) into their websites, and user interactions. Messages about cookies and their data implications immediately popped up with greater frequency. Privacy messages took over the internet.

What is GDPR? In simple terms it's a set of rules as to what data collectors can and cannot do with data collected from users. Under GDPR companies who collect data must describe what its used for, and refrain from using that same data for any other purpose. It proscribes that companies should collect the minimum amount of data required for the purpose, and limit how long they hold on to the data. Internal systems must allow for companies to share with client's what data they hold about them and where & how it's being used– not an inconsequential task given the proliferation of systems within some organizations. GDPR also says if you're going to make an automated decision impacting a client, you've got to be able to explain the logic. When clients come calling to delete their data, organizations must be in a position to do so not just for their own company, but for vendors to their company.

Regulation

Today, post the 2008-2009 Great Recession, regulation abounds in most industries. Issues include consent, profiling, human intervention, General Data Protection Regulation in Europe, privacy, cross boundary/international, approach to customers, compliance, risk assessments, expansion into different markets with their unique regulations, how in-house counsels collaborate, data biases, and the liability of AI products and services.

Bert Kaminski, a Chief Counsel at ServiceMax in the United States, and previously a Chief Counsel at GE, and Assistant General Counsel at Oracle, is recognized as a highly accomplished in-house General Counsel specializing in technology law including data privacy, information security, cloud and all aspects of a corporate practice relevant to a commercial business. Bert was on the Board of Directors of the Association of Corporate Counsel New Jersey Chapter, including a tenure as President of the chapter, a true legal expert on the Cloud, SaaS and industrial IoT, but perhaps most importantly brilliant at adapting new areas of technology to cutting edge principles of the law. Bert was Assistant General Counsel managing the Cloud Services team.

I recall watching Bert and colleagues during the Emerging Legal Issues segment of the Bloomberg Law Forum in May 2018 which reinforced how complex the issue is from a legal perspective. In a subsequent interview, I asked Bert about the primary areas related to AI or related issues being raised by Chief Counsel's within their leadership team especially given the complexity of AI implications. He said "There are two ways I look at AI, commercial offerings, and internal processes. I will be referring to the former. When speaking to business executives about AI offerings within a commercial environment, I emphasize scalability and repeatability to what they do. Standardization of approach, replicate elsewhere. Groups spend a lot of resources to create data models or algorithms. If it becomes too specific, then it can't be applied to other use cases. It becomes important to build scalable things."

Bert continued, "A concern is the risk of a model not working well, where you create each model with big complexity, there is inherent risk of not scaling what has been learned. There's a risk a model could go wrong, and then who would be responsible. Who owns IP rights of AI at large, whoever supplies the dataset owns it, A dataset could be augmented between parties, which then creates new results. What if everyone owns a sliver of it. It ultimately only works if it nets out to clear and distinct ownership. Otherwise it could paralyze projects or opportunities."

As a consultant, your business client will be equally concerned about handling their clients' personal information, and the challenges that raises. Kaminski argues "Assume datasets include personal information. For example, the mobile phone has a unique ID (identifier). The unique ID has to constitute personal information. Gathering data on a communication devices performance and feeding it to the cloud, ie servicing equipment; this raises issues about how you build the datasets. The law requires notice and consent."

When collecting information from a customer, while more may be helpful from a data analysis perspective, less is better from a regulatory perspective. Kaminski continues, "A related topic is data minimization. Machine learning requires robust datasets. GDPR (General Data Protection Regulation) says you collect the minimum information, only for permitted purposes and no longer. One must be careful who you share it with including partners."

AI has been described as a suitcase word, in other words a toolkit. Does the organization have a standard process for legal considerations to map business problems and opportunities to the right tool in the toolkit? This helps other CEO's to understand a best practice approach to take. Some have asked if GDPR is an AI killer (as has Datanami.com). There is a focus on strengthening and unifying data protection for individuals within the EU. Some of the key considerations include:

- Informed consent from the customer, details on the use of profiling (use of personnel characteristics or behaviours to make generalizations about a person).
- Withdrawing consent from profiling algorithms, uncovering potential algorithmic biases, requiring human judgment to be involved in every profiling decision, risk assessments, compliance, transparency with the DOJ, the case of the United States.
- How In-House Counsels and external counsels network and share to keep pace with changes.

- The importance of communication given the stakes are higher.
- And finally as Bert Kaminski predicted at the Bloomberg Law Forum that "technology will outstrip regulation", and "monopolies could starve out smaller entities"

In 2018, I attended the Toronto Tech Summit. The assertion made was that most large organizations in North America have embedded GDPR already. Attending such conferences, tackling business problems around digital transformation, CEO's are driven to a variety of perspectives regarding protecting their core revenues or business platforms. Often, they're asking "Is there any difference in approach from any other priority issue for the company"? "Does pace of change enter into approaching it differently than other priorities?"

As you discuss the topic of privacy and security of personal information, consider the risk aversion of today's business leaders. Bert Kaminski argues "there's a lot of hype about this creating at least two types of results: it may drive CEO's to make decisions that are overly optimistic or could paralyze a CEO if there's a lot of unknowns or risks. AI can be like any other technology except for the feeling of not getting on board quickly enough. In the past, one might have an 18-month advantage before commoditization occurs; with AI that changes."

In the MIT "Artificial Intelligence: Implications for Business Strategy" program, we discussed the collective intelligence of human and machine. From a legal and regulatory perspective, that philosophy enters into the paradigm business leaders need to be mindful of for employees impacted by AI. For example, AI can alleviate repetitive and menial tasks including paperwork, scheduling, boosting productivity. McKinsey's study on employment impact of AI suggested 35-40% of jobs will be impacted in the next 20 years, worldwide upwards of 375 million jobs lost. As such there are ethical aspects of employment relationships including retraining, introducing other jobs, and upstreaming the value of jobs.

One of Kaminski's area of responsibility is GE's Service Max which is an example of a commercial offering whose mission is zero downtime, and zero industrial outage. Corporations can't have a transportation or industrial system go down. Human lives could be affected. Service Max ensures with intelligent systems that maintenance is not time based but is predictive using historical data and machine learning from the equipment in question. Thus, you can have customers own their systems maintenance. It doesn't necessarily reduce jobs, rather ServiceMax provides opportunities for effective redeployment. If you can reduce costs by say 25%, then you can reinvest elsewhere and redeploy engineers leveraging predictive maintenance.

What to Do About It

A valid concern for consumers is that AI may further compromise their data privacy online. In fact, a 2018 study by Genpact found 71% of respondents would rather not use AI, even if it improved the customers experience if it meant risking privacy infringement.

Consumer education, integrity in dealing with customer data, and transparency are key determinants of a responsible data privacy policy. Proving to customers that your firm is as concerned about data security as they are by your actions and communications goes a long way towards building consumer trust. What considerations? Offering easy access to common-sense, simple language policies; investing in data protection capabilities yet dealing quickly, confidently and openly with data breaches; redacting sensitive information where possible; driving compliance within the organization and externally with regulators and certification bodies; teaching consumers about your products, services, policies and AI's impacts on each; and advising consumers when they're speaking to a robot at a call center.

From an organizational protection perspective, there are litany of tools to consider including intrusion detection tools, actively monitoring and analyzing security information for their vulnerable systems, conducting vulnerability assessments, using security information and event management tools, regularly conducting cyber security threat assessments of their systems, subscribing to a threat intelligence service, and engaging in data system penetration testing.

Facebook's so-called "adventure" with Cambridge Analytica's sharing of consumer information should be a cautionary tale for all organizations. Mark Zuckerberg, CEO, publicly expressed his regret over that situation, acknowledging blame for not taking a broad enough view of Facebook's responsibilities to consumers. Yet Facebook survives and thrives, so understanding the approach they took in getting their CEO out in front of the media and regulators arguably eventually assuaged the potential pitfalls.

15

How Buying Is Changing in 2019

One of the most compelling sources of business research in the world is Gartner. If you've never heard Brent Adamson, Distinguished Vice President, with the research firm, frankly you're missing out. Brent leads the sales practice at Gartner and has been studying sales and buying behaviours for years. In a recent webinar, he pointed out that things are changing in the buying process, and if you're not in tune with the changes, you could be wasting valuable time. Oh, and yes AI can play a role!

It starts with the number of people involved in the buying process. For years it was approximately 5.45 people. In 2019, that number has risen to 9-10 people. Within the same company. How's that possible? Well let's consider the business leader, finance, IT, procurement, compliance, privacy, legal, risk, sales, marketing. Each of them is doing their own research of sorts; 4-5 sources each. Then sources conflict, so a de-conflicting activity begins (my whitepaper versus yours, my sources vs yours) or 15% of the total time to get to a single version of the "truth". The buying process is taking longer.

The word truth is in quotations because the world is "awash in quality information where 89% of customers in a Gartner survey said that information was generally of high quality". As a consultant or information source, it is much more difficult to stand out. Being a thought leader is no longer unique. So now customers have difficulty knowing what to believe. There's a plethora of solid information, in fact, so much so that it can be overwhelming for customers.

What customers want, according to Adamson, is information that will specifically help them make progress (advance) because it's so overwhelming and not linear. B2B buying is about completion since it's not really linear progress. Since that's true, sales processes should be really a buying process given the order is more simultaneous than linear, and the emphasis should be on the buyers activities.

The complexity of the buying process is so overwhelming that a tool is needed to address every step, to reduce the overwhelming complexity for each stakeholder. One can use AI to fast-track research in decision-making. One can investigate hundreds of sources and have the AI make buying recommendations. AI can and will do this for you in the future.

16

The Future

"Success in creating Artificial Intelligence would be the biggest event in human history. Unfortunately, it might also be the last unless we learn how to avoid the risks" – Stephen Hawking.

A trillion dollars is a huge sum of money. By 2022, the Internet of Things (IoT) is expected to achieve that level of savings for industry and individuals alike through transparent and immersive experiences according to Gartner.

So, what does the present have in store for AI? Well we start with the "year of the voice". People are increasingly turning from texting to talking. With the advent of hyper accuracy in voice recognition (think back a decade when your voice recognition software was less than 50% accurate) voice input systems are now viable. Alexa from Amazon has become prolific in advertisements, and television shows where it's featured interacting with homeowners. Alexa is expanding "her" service offering beyond dimming the lights, playing music and offering restaurant recommendations.

In fact, organizations like Adobe and Salesforce are branching into omnichannel capabilities with voice moving to the forefront. Customer service contact centers are leveraging greater, deeper upfront interactions with more human-like responses, incorporating emotional understanding such as customer frustration. I recently called Apple Care for what was described as an unusual situation where my MacBook was not booting up and none of the traditional solutions worked. Once I vented to the "silicon receptionist" I was moved quickly to a human agent. Great combination of automation and human interaction.

Want to frustrate a fraudster? Make them try to do something with voice data. In 2019, it's not much. So, your bank and telephone company are leveraging this biometric tech. In fact, using only a small sample of words of speech, voice biometrics can identify you, including whether the speech is live or not, so that fraudsters cannot leverage recordings in the case of a breach. My last contact with my bank customer service center started with them offering me to change my password. Not from one alphanumeric password to another. Rather my voice became my password. The uniqueness of my voice now serves to introduce me to my banker as the "real me". As the world continues to experience record levels of hacking, your real-time voice may be your best safety measure.

In 2017, brands like Best Buy and Walmart entered into relationships with Google Home and Amazon Alexa to increase the adoption of voice-based software solutions and services. Successful marketers are thinking like those in customer care in dealing with a variety of customers at point of contact professionals. Once organizations gain customers' trust, they can begin achieving the cost-efficiencies voice solutions bring. When I recently used Google assistant to find out who was winning the Tour de France, I simply asked the question verbally. After receiving the response (a series of news articles to click on), I responded with a "Thank you". Google Assistant said, " merci beaucoup". Not bad for a bunch of wires and algorithms!

Elon Musk & His Predictions

Not long ago, Elon Musk, of Tesla, SpaceX and Boring Company fame, made a series of predictions regarding the future. His predictions ranged from the eventuality of pervasive electric and autonomous vehicles to tunnel transportation to Mars landings. As of writing this book, Tesla production and delivery is ramping up, SpaceX launches are commonplace, and Hyperloop competitions for tunneling abound. It's clear Musk has a wildly substantial impact on the world of 2019, and his predictions suggest a future of more of the same.

Cars becoming "all-electric" in 2019 doesn't seem so far-fetched, but aircraft, and ships as well? Musk thinks so "with the ironic exception of rockets". Getting back to cars, he says half of all cars will be electric by 2027.

Picture yourself in 2028. If you're still driving around in your fossil-fuel engined 2018 Mustang GT, will people look at you as if you're riding a horse? Musk thinks so. Maybe you're too sentimental to give up that "horse".

What about jobs and human income? Musk argued at the World Government Summit in Dubai that automation will lead to "fewer jobs that a robot cannot do better". UBI or Universal Basic Income is on the horizon for humanity, as well, according to Musk, despite some recent failures in Scandinavia.

How about that vacation to Mars? You'll have to wait until at least 2025 when the first human explorers are predicted to travel to, and land on Mars, according to Musk speaking at the International Astronautical Congress

If you'd like to live in Montreal but work in Toronto, Canada, it takes about 5 hours to do the "commute". In fact, it can take over an hour just to get to Toronto from a suburb of the same city. Yet with a Hyperloop tunnel that time frame could be 25 minutes from Montreal. Not bad. Getting out of bed in your Montreal home at 7 and having your morning coffee at your desk in Toronto before 8 o'clock. With a network of tunnels, North America could be your playground if you use Hyperloop to get to and from work.

Sounds generally positive, does it not? Well, "not" would be the correct answer. Musk has stated his belief that AI is more dangerous than nuclear weapons, in fact it's the biggest risk to civilization. Given the competition for AI dominance, Musk can't be faulted for thinking this way.

To go a step further, artificial intelligence algorithms (deep intelligence) placed inside robots with greater than simple, "narrow" AI embedded in them, contain as much a risk of doing harm as good. Musk believes it's the former according to his speech at the National Governor's Association.

At the same Dubai World Government Summit, Musk argued that to merely survive, humans will need to become part robot. The merger of biological and digital intelligence and form may not be that far away. For the disabled, new technologies and components, attached to or embedded under human skin are making it possible to walk, talk, throw and more. Is it such a stretch to think of able bodied humans injecting chips into their skin as monitors? That would be just the start. If we can manage matching the brains bandwidth, it could be possible to merge humans and digital components together.

5G

Imagine connectivity speeds of 100 times faster than the widely available 4G standard today. Download times reduced substantially such as full movies downloaded in seconds, and incredible responsiveness for your applications. Telecom companies are in a race to become your 5G provider. Billions in 5G infrastructure spending is occurring right now to offer subscribers lightning fast connectivity.

So what is 5G? It is the 5th generation of mobile networks, a massive change from 4G LTE as measured by latency (the time taken for devices to respond to each other over the wireless network). 3G networks typical response time was 100 milliseconds, 4G is approximately 30 milliseconds and 5G is expected to be as low as 1 millisecond.

For AI-powered offerings augmented with 5G, think autonomous vehicles, and the ability to increase the connection speed of data flowing between the vehicle and data sources. Where more reliable coverage is needed, including machine downtime and IoT sensors, AI and 5G are a marriage made in heaven. Smart city technologies will depend upon the combination of AI smarts, and 5G speed.

Quantum Computers

Today's fastest supercomputer (as of writing) is called Summit and is housed at Oak Ridge National Lab in Tennessee. Two tennis courts in area, Summit is currently being used to run deep learning algorithms at a billion billion operations per second to work on one of the primary challenges of our time, climate change.

Quantum computing operates or is expected to operate with all levels of artificial intelligence be they narrow, general, super intelligence, or "compassionate" artificial super intelligence. Yet quantum computing is quite fragile with sensitivity to environmental noise from outside the device like temperature (-460 degrees Fahrenheit), requiring highly specialized techniques to preserve the quantum state. It's unlikely the majority of organizations would ever have a quantum computer, rather the environment would be more like a cloud system with clients buying access. Quantum computing operations are occurring today in companies like Intel, IBM, Microsoft and Google with capabilities (as measured by units called qubits) from 5 to 50 qubits.

You may have heard or read about quantum computers, and their potential to support the processing needs of machine learning, neural networks and algorithms. Or not. Artificial intelligence as it approaches General AI (higher level super-intelligent systems) requires many things including vast amounts of processing power. Yet we are still years away from a full-fledged true quantum computer.

The 5G and quantum-powered future, though, is coming.

17

Conclusion

We started on this journey talking about AI's evolution. Today is merely a point in time. Over the next decade, equilibrium will be reached in the execution of artificial intelligence by human leaders, executives, and board members. Consultants have an important role to play in that evolution as CEO's and business owners, to this point at least, have demonstrated their hesitation in implementing AI, and making it a part of the organizational culture.

By reading this book, you've demonstrated, at a minimum, your openness to the potential of artificial intelligence in the business world. Since the 1950's there have been at least four AI winters, but this era is different. Different because of computer speed, storage in the cloud, availability of vast amounts of data (as previously mentioned 90% being created in the last two years), high levels of investment globally, and an increasing awareness off the benefits of AI beyond commercial applications.

Business leaders and consultants, in particular early adopters, have an incredible opportunity today. Given the speed of AI adoption by pioneers, they are leaping ahead of the competition, and the lead just may be insurmountable. Consultants can share their knowledge, provide insights to business leaders, reduce the time to economic scale, and minimize the risks of unsuccessful AI integration for their clients. Not to mention how consultants can use AI within their own business conducting research, writing reports, scheduling meetings, composing emails, developing prospects and so much more.

If you've read this far, continue reading from other sources. Make it part of your everyday activities. There is so much to know about AI, and it's accelerating daily. Find ways to keep current, and it will pay dividends for your firm, and your client's business. Buckle your seat belt for what will be an incredible ride.

Brian Lenahan, Toronto, Canada 2019

A Quick Favor Please?

Before you go may I ask you for a quick favor?

Good, I knew I could count on you.

Would you please leave this book a review on Amazon?

Reviews are very important for authors, as they help us sell more books. This will in turn enable me to write more books for you.

Please take a quick minute to go to Amazon.com or Amazon.ca, type in the books title and leave this book an honest review. I promise it doesn't take very long, but it can help this book reach more readers just like you.

Thank you for reading and thank you so much for being part of the journey.

-Brian

APPENDIX – Definitions

AI can be segmented by function including machine learning, decision making, natural language processing, responding, computer vision and hearing:

- **Machine Learning** (ML) can include recommendation engines (like Netflix), data mining, deep learning, reinforcement learning, supervised and unsupervised learning. Machine Learning is the science of enabling computers to learn and act like we do, learning over time, on their own (autonomously) much the way we do. Humans learn through stories, facts, memory, and experiences. Computers take in data (historic pictures of dogs and cats for example) and then through ML form conclusions (it's a cat or a dog).

- **Deep Learning** is a subset of ML where algorithms leverage those neural networks we spoke about earlier (in this case the digital kind). Given some early success with deep learning, it is increasingly a preferred way to train computers especially where the activities are complex and have extremely large data sets. Mimicking the human brain to some shallow degree, deep learning learns through trial and error much like animals do.

- **Deep Neural Networks** are actually quite simple. You pose a question like is the animal in this picture a cat or a dog. By starting with an input layer of millions of images of dogs and cats injected into an algorithm, processed millions of times, there is an output layer with a probability factor that this is a dog or a cat.

- **Supervised Learning** – Where data can be labeled, this is an effective way for a machine to learn a function from labeled training data.

- **Unsupervised Learning** – Most of the world's data (over 90%) has been produced in the last two years, and most of that data is unstructured, in other words not labeled, so a different approach to training computers was required. Unsupervised learning draws inferences from datasets finding hidden patterns or grouping in data.

- **Cognitive Computing** – often used as a synonym for AI, is slightly different in that it generally provides information for a human to solve a problem and stops short of providing the solution itself. The concepts overlap in many ways, however, as cognitive computing is based on the simulation of human processes in a computerized model. Like AI, it involves self-learning systems that use data mining, pattern recognition, and natural language processing

- **Classification** – this process allows computers to understand to which category a piece or set of data belongs.

- **Regression** – A statistical technique for estimating the relationships among variables (includes linear regression, logistic regression, and other approaches)

- **Algorithm** – A self-contained step-by-step set of operations to be performed. Algorithms perform calculation, data processing, and/or automated reasoning tasks.

- **Decision-Making** – can include case-based reasoning and expert systems

- **Computer Vision** (CV) and hearing – includes facial & gesture recognition, handwriting recognition, optical character recognition, image & video recognition, and speech recognition. CV attempts to optimize the vision capability of a computer or machine. It takes one or more images and enhances information extraction from them.

- **Natural Language Processing or NLP** – includes natural language understanding, programming. sentiment analysis and machine translation. NLP gives computers the ability to comprehend human speech, whether written or spoken. The most well-known examples today are Apple's Siri, Google assistant, and Amazon's Alexa. Another example is the ability to summarize a set of documents (this is one of my favourites as a consummate researcher and curiousity geek). NLP permits review of millions of documents, and natural language generation can then create summary reports from all of that information. Potara is a multi-document summarization system that uses NLP.

- **Robotics** – often used in dangerous environments like bomb detection, manufacturing, or space exploration, robots can simply be automation or can take human form helping the acceptance of a robot in activities usually performed by people. Robots can replicate walking, lifting, speech, cognition, and more as advances are made.

About the Author

Brian Lenahan is an Artificial Intelligence Strategist & Innovation Speed expert having received his Artificial Intelligence training at the Massachusetts Institute of Technology (MIT) Sloan School of Management (Cambridge, MA). During a 22-year career, including executive roles at a Fortune 500 Bank in US and Canada, his consistent career thread has been innovation.

Leading multimillion-dollar programs, and teams of over 150 employees in the US, Canada and partnering with resources in India, Brian understands the demands of leadership. He has experience in numerous industries including Financial Services, Computer Services, Transportation, and Real Estate as well as functions including Strategy, IT, HR, Operations, Learning, and Financial Crimes & Fraud Management. He has consulted to C-Suite, and Senior Management leaders for over 15 years.

Brian Lenahan is a recognized keynote speaker and a developer of AI training programs for a national consulting association. He is the CEO of Aquitaine Innovation Advisors (an AI consulting firm) and the Chief Strategy Officer & CFO of Rainmaker, a Canadian tech startup in the Sales domain. Brian's experience skydiving, parasailing, zip lining canyons, and running half-marathons led to his personal approach of balancing prudent risk-taking while still seeking out commercial opportunities.

Brian is currently pursuing his Doctorate in Innovation & Strategy and is focused on designing and developing Artificial Intelligence learning tools for consultants, coaches, students, business leaders and entrepreneurs.

NOTES

Why This Book and Why Now?

1. Deloitte. "The Fourth Industrial Revolution is here—are you ready?" https://www2.deloitte.com/content/dam/Deloitte/tr/Documents/manufacturing/Industry4-0_Are-you-ready_Report.pdf 2018.

2. Gartner. "Top 10 strategic trends of Internet of Things (IoT) for 2019". https://www.gartner.com/.../2018-11-07-gartner-identifies-top-10-strategic-iot-technologies-and-trends

3. PwC's 21st Annual Global CEO Survey, https://www.pwc.com/gx/en/ceo-agenda/ceosurvey/2018/gx.html

Chapter 1

1. Popular Science Magazine. 2018. The Brain. https://www.amazon.com/POPULAR-SCIENCE-Your-New-Brain/dp/1547845147

2. Dr. Suzana Herculano-Houzel. How many neurons make a human brain? Billions fewer than we thought. The Guardian Newspaper. February 28, 2012. https://www.theguardian.com/science/blog/2012/feb/28/how-many-neurons-human-brain

3. Geoffrey Hinton. How a Toronto professor's research revolutionized artificial intelligence. https://www.thestar.com/news/world/2015/04/17/how-a-toronto-professors-research-revolutionized-artificial-intelligence.html

4. Pedro Domingos. "The Master Algorithm: How the Quest for the Ultimate Learning Machine Will Remake Our World." https://machinelearnings.co/the-master-algorithm-15e27cec2d4d

5. Peter Nowak. "The ethical dilemmas of self-driving cars." Globe and Mail. February 2, 2018 https://www.theglobeandmail.com/globe-drive/culture/technology/the-ethical-dilemmas-of-self-drivingcars/article37803470/

6. Markets and Markets. "Natural Language Processing Market worth 16.07 Billion USD by 2021" https://www.marketsandmarkets.com/PressReleases/natural-language-processing-nlp.asp

7. ZMEScience.com. "Researchers quantify basic rules of ethics and morality, plan to copy them into smart cars, even AI." https://www.zmescience.com/science/smart-cars-ai-ethics/ 2017 - Proof there are scenarios where machines perform better than humans

8. Gartner. "Disruptive Technologies Approaching a Tipping Point".

https://demo.idg.com.au/nzcio/cio100/2018/Auckland%2 0-%20Michele%20Caminos.pdf

9. Deloitte. Deloitte Global CEO Study 2019. https://www2.deloitte.com/global/en/pages/about-deloitte/articles/davos-insights.html

10. PwC. PwC Global CEO Study 2019. https://www.pwc.com/gx/en/ceo-agenda/ceosurvey/2019/ca

11. South China Morning Post. "MIT invests US$1 billion in AI-focused College of Computing hot on the heels of Tsinghua's AI centre." https//:www.scmp.com/tech/innovation/article/2168746/ mit-invests-us1-billion-ai-focused-college-computing-hot-heels

12. World Economic Forum. January 2019. https://www.youtube.com/watch?v=js4gPN7WST8

13. Vistage Worldwide. Vistage-releases-report-on-small-businesses-and-artificial intelligence. Sept 25, 2018. https://www.vistage.com/press-center/press-release/ https://www.prnewswire.com/.../vistage-releases-report-on-small-businesses-and-artificial-intelligence.

Chapter 2

1. CNBC. "Google CEO: A.I. is more important than fire or electricity". https://www.cnbc.com/2018/02/01/google-

ceo-sundar-pichai-ai-is-more-important-than-fire-electricity.html

2. Geoff Hinton.
   adsabs.harvard.edu/abs/1986Natur.323.533R

3. NPR. "What Does Losing To A Computer Tell Us About Pride?"
   https://www.npr.org/templates/transcript/transcript.php?storyId=379183540

4. TechCrunch.com. "Microsoft CEO Satya Nadella's New Book is More Business Text Than Memoir." https://techcrunch.com/2017/09/25/microsoft-ceo-satya-nadellas-new-book-is-more-business-text-than-memoir/

Chapter 3

1. Harvard Business Review. "What is Disruptive Innovation?" December 2015.
   https://hbr.org/2015/12/what-is-disruptive-innovation

2. Accenture PLC. "Banks' Revenue Growth at Risk Due to Unprecedented Competitive Pressure Resulting from Digital Disruption" October 2018.
   https://newsroom.accenture.com/news/banks-revenue-growth-at-risk-due-to-unprecedented-competitive-pressure-resulting-from-digital-disruption-accenture-study-finds.htm

3. Financial Times. "Google and Facebook dominance forecast to rise". December, 2017.

https://www.ft.com/content/cf362186-d840-11e7-a039-c64b1c09b482

4. Ernst & Young. EY CEO Imperative 2017. https://www.ey.com/en_gl/digital/how-can-you-be-both-the-disruptor-and-the-disrupted

5. KPMG. "KPMG CEO Global Outlook 2017" https://home.kpmg/ca/en/home/insights/2017/06/canadian-ceo-outlook-2017.html

6. KPMG. "KPMG CEO Global Outlook 2018". https://assets.kpmg/content/dam/kpmg/pe/pdf/Publicaciones/Estudios-encuestas/CEO-Outlook-2018-GLOBAL.pdf

7. Harvard Business School. Clayton Christensen's "How Will You Measure Your Life?" https://hbswk.hbs.edu/item/clayton-christensens-how-will-you-measure-your-life

8. Forester. "Predictions 2017: Security And Skills Will Temper Growth Of IoT", 2017. https://www.forrester.com/report/Predictions+2017+Security+And+Skills+Will+Temper+Growth+Of+IoT/-/E-RES136255

9. Global Center for Digital Business Transformation. "Digital Vortex". https://www.cisco.com/c/dam/en/us/solutions/collateral/industry-solutions/digital-vortex-report.pdf

10. Visual Capitalist. "2018 Internet Minute."
    https://www.visualcapitalist.com/internet-minute-2018/

11. Intel. https://www.intel.com/content/www/us/en/internet-of-things/infographics/guide-to-iot.html

Chapter 4

1. Bill Gates. "The Road Ahead". Viking USA; First Edition edition (Oct. 1 1995)

2. CB Insights. "Fintech Trends 2019" https://www.cbinsights.com/research/report/fintech-trends-2019/

3. Visual Capitalist. "Most Valuable U.S. Companies Over 100 Years." https://www.visualcapitalist.com/most-valuable-companies-100-years/. 2017

4. Forbes. "How Much Data Do We Create Every Day? The Mind-Blowing Stats Everyone Should Read." https://www.forbes.com/sites/bernardmarr/2018/05/21/how-much-data-do-we-create-every-day-the-mind-blowing-stats-everyone-should-read/#4da63a4d60ba

5. Visual Capitalist. "2018 Internet Minute". https://www.visualcapitalist.com/internet-minute-2018/

6. Data Reportal. DIGITAL 2019: Q2 GLOBAL DIGITAL STATSHOT. https://datareportal.com/reports/digital-2019-q2-global-digital-statshot

7. Sloan Review. "BCG & MIT Sloan Management Review 2017". https://sloanreview.mit.edu/projects/reshaping-business-with-artificial-intelligence/

8. Capgemini Consulting. "Artificial Intelligence - Where and How to Invest" https://www.capgemini.com/resources/artificial-intelligence-where-and-how-to-invest/)

Chapter 5

1. The Straits Times. "In Davos, US executives warn that China is winning the AI race" https://www.straitstimes.com/world/europe/in-davos-us-executives-warn-that-china-is-winning-the-ai-race

2. Kevin Kelly. "The Three Breakthroughs That Have Finally Unleashed AI on the World." Wired. https://www.wired.com/2014/10/future-of-artificial-intelligence/

3. Joe Galvin. "Research Center". https://www.vistage.com/research-center/author/jgalvin/ Vistage Worldwide.

4. PR Newswire. "Bluewolf." Jan. 12, 2017. https://www.prnewswire.com/news-releases/bluewolf-launches-bluewolf-go-consulting-reimagined-to-get-companies-live-on-salesforce-in-weeks-300389927.html

5. Business Talent Group. "2019 High End Talent Report." https://resources.businesstalentgroup.com/the-2019-high-end-independent-talent-report

Chapter 6

1. McKinsey. "The best response to digital disruption." https://www.mckinsey.com/mgi/overview/in-the-news/the-right-response-to-digital-disruption

2. Fast Company. How to Make Decisions More Efficiently. https://www.fastcompany.com/3049164/how-to-make-decisions-more-efficiently

3. GuruFocus. "Goldman Adds Dr. Pepper to Its Dividend Basket." https://www.gurufocus.com/news/337097/goldman-adds-dr-pepper-to-its-dividend-basket/

4. Thomas J. Watson. "Famous Quotes." https://www.quotes.net/quote/58039

Chapter 7

1. Larry Boyer, "The Robot in the Next Cubicle: What You Need to Know to Adapt and Succeed in the Automation Age". https://www.amazon.com/Robot-Next-Cubicle-Succeed-Automation/dp/1633884090

2. Harvard Business Review. "The Value of Keeping the Right Customers" October 2014.

https://hbr.org/2014/10/the-value-of-keeping-the-right-customers

3. Michelle Moore. SVP, Global Product Development - LHH Knightsbridge. Interview.

4. Edwin Suarez, Director HR, Mobile Oil Corporation. Interview.

5. LinkedIn. 2018 Workplace Learning Report. https://learning.linkedin.com/resources/workplace-learning-report-2018

6. Accenture PLC. "Boost Your AIQ - Transforming Into An AI Business" 2017. https://www.accenture.com/t20170614T050454__w__/us-en/_acnmedia/Accenture/next-gen-5/event-g20-yea-summit/pdfs/Accenture-Boost-Your-AIQ.pdf

7. PwC. 22nd Annual Global CEO Survey. https://www.pwc.com/gx/en/ceo-survey/2019/report/pwc-22nd-annual-global-ceo-survey.pdf

8. World Economic Forum. 4 ways the rise of the machines can work for humans. Jan 9 2018. https://www.weforum.org/agenda/2018/01/how-to-make-the-rise-of-themachines-work-for-humans/

9. Boston Globe. Scott Santens. " Robots Will Take Your Job," https://www.bostonglobe.com/ideas/2016/02/04/robots-will-take-you-job/

10. Daron Acemoglu, Pascual Restrepo. "Robots and Jobs: Evidence from US Labor Markets." https://economics.mit.edu/files/15254

Chapter 8

1. BCG. "Putting Artificial Intelligence to Work". February 2018 www.sipotra.it/wp-content/uploads/2018/02/Putting-Artificial-Intelligence-to-Work.pdf

2. McKinsey & Company. "Where Machines Could Replace Humans and Where They Can't" July 2016. https://www.mckinsey.com/business-functions/digital-mckinsey/our-insights/where-machines-could-replace-humans-and-where-they-cant-yet

3. BCG & MIT Sloan Management Review 2017. https://sloanreview.mit.edu/projects/reshaping-business-with-artificial-intelligence/

4. BCG & MIT Sloan Management Review 2017 "Artificial Intelligence in Business Gets Real," https://globenewswire.com/news-release/2018/09/17/1572080/0/en/MIT-Sloan-Management-Review-and-Boston-Consulting-Group-Study-Dispels-Five-Major-Myths-About-Artificial-Intelligence.html

5. Statista. Reason's for Adopting AI Worldwide 2017. https://www.statista.com/statistics/747775/worldwide-reasons-for-adopting-ai/

6. British Telecom and The Economist Intelligence Unit. September 2017. https://www.globalservices.bt.com/en/aboutus/news-press/digital-transformation-top-priority-for-ceos

7. PwC. 22nd Global CEO Survey. https://www.pwc.com/gx/en/ceo-agenda/ceosurvey/2019/gx.html

8. Irish Times, "The top six trends in artificial intelligence for 2019" https://www.irishtimes.com/business/technology/the-top-six-trends-in-artificial-intelligence-for-2019-1.3751459

Chapter 9

1. Dr. Ben Waber, PhD, MIT and CEO of Humanyze. https://web.media.mit.edu/~bwaber/

2. Dr. Charles Martin, PhD, University of Chicago and CEO, Calculation Consulting. https://emerj.com/ai-podcast-interviews/machine-learning-still-getting-sea-legs-in-world-of-midsize-business-a-conversation-with-charles-martin/

Chapter 10

1. Cortex 2014, Gartner 2016, AI-IA 2017. Automation failures.

2. New York Times. "Self-Driving Uber Car Kills Pedestrian In Arizona Where Robots Roam." March 2018. https://www.nytimes.com/2018/03/19/technology/uber-driverless-fatality.html

3. Synced. "2018 in Review: 10 Failures" https://syncedreview.com/2018/12/10/2018-in-review-10-ai-failures/

4. Gartner. "Trends Emerge in the Gartner Hype Cycle for Emerging Technologies." 2018. https://www.gartner.com/smarterwithgartner/5-trends-emerge-in-gartner-hype-cycle-for-emerging-technologies-2018/

Chapter 11

1. Gartner. "Gartner Says AI Technologies Will Be in Almost Every New Software Product by 2020 https://www.gartner.com/en/newsroom/press-releases/2017-07-18-gartner-says-ai-technologies-will-be-in-almost-every-new-software-product-by-2020

2. Judson Althoff. "It's Time For The CEO To Own AI As A Strategic Imperative." Chief Executive.Net. May

2018. https://chiefexecutive.net/its-time-for-the-ceo-to-own-ai-as-a-strategic-imperative/

3. Gijs Van Wulfen. "Organizations frustrate their most innovative employees". LinkedIn post.

4. MIT Sloan Management Review. "Artificial Intelligence in Business Gets Real," https://globenewswire.com/news-release/2018/09/17/1572080/0/en/MIT-Sloan-Management-Review-and-Boston-Consulting-Group-Study-Dispels-Five-Major-Myths-About-Artificial-Intelligence.html

5. Ernst & Young. "EY CEO Imperative 2017 – How Can You Be Both the Disruptor and the Disrupted?" https://www.ey.com/en_gl/digital/how-can-you-be-both-the-disruptor-and-the-disrupted

6. IDC. "Estimates on corporate spending on AI." https://www.idc.com/getdoc.jsp?containerId=prUS44291818

7. Gartner. "Disruptive Technologies Approaching a Tipping Point". https://demo.idg.com.au/nzcio/cio100/2018/Auckland%20-%20Michele%20Caminos.pdf

8. KPMG. "CEO Global Outlook 2017" https://home.kpmg/ca/en/home/insights/2017/06/canadian-ceo-outlook-2017.html

9. Deloitte. "The Fourth Industrial Revolution is here—are you ready?"

https://www2.deloitte.com/content/dam/Deloitte/tr/Documents/manufacturing/Industry4-0_Are-you-ready_Report.pdf 2018

10. PwC's 21st Annual Global CEO Survey, https://www.pwc.com/gx/en/ceo-agenda/ceosurvey/2018/gx.html

11. Edwin Suarez, Director HR, Mobile oil Corporation. Interview.

Chapter 12

1. Gartner. "Gartner CEO's and Senior Executives Survey 2018." https://www.gartner.com/en/newsroom/press-releases/2018-05-01-gartner-survey-reveals-that-ceo-priorities-are-shifting-to-embrace-digital-business

2. Chatbot Magazine. "Afraid of AI? Part 2/3: Repeated Optimization, Not Elimination". https://chatbotsmagazine.com/afraid-of-ai-part-2-3-repeated-optimization-not-elimination-4cc9e2dca7bb

3. Professor Donald Sull. MIT Management – Executive education. https://executive.mit.edu/faculty/profile/295-donald-sull

4. CB Insights. "Fintech Trends 2019" https://www.cbinsights.com/research/report/fintech-trends-2019/

5. IDC. "Estimates on corporate spending on AI." https://www.idc.com/getdoc.jsp?containerId=prUS44291818

6. Fortune.com. "Automation Jobs Will Put 10,000 to Work." https://www.fortune.com/2017/05/01/automation-jobs-will-put-1000-humans-to-work-study-says/

7. PwC's 21st Annual Global CEO Survey, https://www.pwc.com/gx/en/ceo-agenda/ceosurvey/2018/gx.html

8. World Economic Forum. "The Future of Jobs Report 2018." http://www3.weforum.org/docs/WEF_Future_of_Jobs_2018.pdf

9. BCG. "Profiting from Personalization." May 2017. https://www.bcg.com/en-ca/publications/2017/retail-marketing-sales-profiting-personalization.aspx

Chapter 13

1. The Economist. "The Construction Industry Productivity Problem." (https://www.economist.com/leaders/2017/08/17/the-construction-industrys-productivity-problem)

2. McKinsey. "Improving construction productivity." https://www.mckinsey.com/industries/capital-

projects-and-infrastructure/our-insights/improving-construction-productivity July 2017.

3. UK Government. "Construction 2025: strategy. Joint strategy from government and industry for the future of the UK construction industry." www.gov.uk/government/publications/construction-2025-strategy'. 2013.

4. The Diplomat. "Japan Open Doors for More Foreign Workers" https://thediplomat.com/2018/06/japan-open-doors-for-more-foreign-workers/

5. Boston Consultancy Group. "BIM Revolutions Comes to Building Materials." https://www.bcg.com/publications/2017/process-industries-engineered-products-bim-revolution-comes-building-materials.aspx February 2017.

6. Magoutech.com "U.S. Construction Industry Trends: Beyond Digital Transformation" https://magoutech.com/u-s-construction-industry-trends-beyond-digital-transformation/

7. PRNewswire. "Amazon Outpaces Total Market Growth in U.S. Sales of Household Items" prnewswire.com/news-releases/amazon-outpaces-total-market-growth-in-us-sales-of-household-items-300436048.html

8. McKinsey. "Commercial drones are here: The future of unmanned aerial systems" December 2017.

https://www.mckinsey.com/industries/capital-projects-and-infrastructure/our-insights/commercial-drones-are-here-the-future-of-unmanned-aerial-systems

9. VOA News. "World Economic Forum 5 million jobs are expected to be lost by 2020" (https://learningenglish.voanews.com/a/robots-change-construction-industry/4310601.html)

10. ISG. "Engineering and Construction Firm Leverages RPA to Transform Billing Operations" (http://isg-one.com/related-case-studies-detail/engineering-and-construction-firm-leverages-rpa-to-transform-billing-operations)

Chapter 14

1. Bert Kaminski, Chief Counsel, ServiceMax. Interview. 2018

2. Bloomberg Law Forum. "Emerging Legal Issues" video. May 2018

3. Toronto Tech Summit 2018. The assertion made was that most large organizations in North America have embedded GDPR already.

4. MIT. "Artificial Intelligence: Implications for Business Strategy" program. Online Course. 2018

5. McKinsey. "Jobs Lost, Jobs Gained: Workforce transition in a time of automation." December 2017. https://www.mckinsey.com/~/media/mckinsey/featured%20insights/future%20of%20organizations/what%20the%20future%20of%20work%20will%20mean%20for%20jobs%20skills%20and%20wages/mgi-jobs-lost-jobs-gained-report-december-6-2017.ashx lost, the ethical aspects of employment relationships including

6. BankInfo Security.com. "US Data Breaches Hit All-Time High" February 2018 https://bankinfosecurity.com/us-data-breaches-hit-all-time-high-a-10622,

7. Genpact. "The consumer: Sees AI benefits but still prefers the human touch." https://www.genpact.com/downloadable-content/the-consumer-sees-ai-benefits-but-still-prefers-the-human-touch.pdf

Chapter 15

1. Gartner, Inc., "Adjust Selling to 2019's Buying Realities" webinar. Brent Adamson, Distinguished Vice President. Feb, 2019.

Chapter 16

1. Gartner. "Gartner Says 8.4 Billion Connected 'Things' Will Be in Use in 2017, Up 31 Percent From 2016"

https://www.gartner.com/en/newsroom/press-releases/2017-02-07-gartner-says-8-billion-connected-things-will-be-in-use-in-2017-up-31-percent-from-2016

2. Branden, John. "Why Elon Musk says 50% of all cars will be electric by 2027" https://www.computerworld.com/article/3208036/why-elon-musk-says-50-of-all-cars-will-be-electric-by-2027.html.

3. Thompson, Cadie. "11 wild predictions Elon Musk has made about the future." Business Insider. https://www.businessinsider.com/elon-musk-predictions-2017-8

4. Vincent, James. "Elon Musk says we need to regulate AI before it becomes a danger to humanity." The Verge. https://www.theverge.com/2017/7/17/15980954/elon-musk-ai-regulation-existential-threat

5. Simonite, Tom. "The World's Fastest Supercomputer Breaks an AI Record". January 31, 2019. Wired. https://www.wired.com/story/worlds-fastest-supercomputer-breaks-ai-record/

Chapter 17

1. Marr, Bernard. "How Much Data Do We Create Every Day? The Mind-Blowing Stats Everyone Should Read" https://www.forbes.com/sites/bernardmarr/2018/05/21/ho

w-much-data-do-we-create-every-day-the-mind-blowing-
stats-everyone-should-read/#7151d0b660b

INDEX

Netflix, 22, 28
neural networks, 18, 22, 36, 61, 254
neurons, 18, 36
Nvidia, 57

O

Optimum Speed, 109, 110, 114, 115, 116, 117, 130
Outreach.io, 100

P

pattern, 24, 156, 171, 173
pattern recognition, 24, 156, 171
Paysa, 199
Peter Drucker, 112
pioneers, 14, 159, 164, 165, 191, 257
Popular Science, 18, 259
prediction, 81, 178, 193, 239
Predictive Analytics, 99
privacy, 160, 230, 232, 233, 235, 240, 242, 245
processing speed, 19
PwC, 15, 43, 96, 138, 166, 191, 203, 204, 259, 261, 270, 275, 277

Q

Quantum Computers, 254
Quill, 100

R

recommendations, 85, 249
Recruitment, 80, 81
Regression, 24
reinforcement learning, 22, 28, 37, 48, 169
robotics, 9, 156, 204, 205, 222, 223, 224
Robotics, 26, 42, 210, 222
robots, 26, 42, 55, 58, 87, 135, 222, 226, 253, 279
RPA, 155, 156, 225

S

SaaS, 162, 163, 235
Salesforce, 97, 98, 198, 249
Salesforce AppExchange, 98

Sentiment analysis, 84
Siri, 26, 34, 50, 69
Sloan School of Management, 11
smart, 29, 50, 68, 71, 210, 211, 215, 261
smart cities, 210
SMB, 45
Snapchat, 77
Software Advice, 98
Software-as-a-Service, 162
Sotheby's, 29
SpaceX, 57, 251
Speech recognition, 33
Speed, 11, 77, 109, 111, 112, 114, 116, 118, 121
Stephen Hawking, 248
Supervised Learning, 23
synapses, 18

T

Tesla, 251
tools, 8, 10, 12, 15, 61, 70, 84, 88, 89, 90, 95, 98, 99, 159, 217, 219, 243

U

Uber, 57, 77, 177, 273
Unsupervised Learning, 23

V

Vector, 15, 48
Virtual Reality, 69, 214, 215
voice, 33, 52, 69, 230, 248, 249, 250

W

Watson, 49, 50, 130, 177, 268
Waymo, 32
winter, 48
World Economic Forum, 44, 147, 204, 223, 270, 279

Y

YouTube, 5, 62, 64, 77

Z

Zoom.ai, 100